I0474599

True Love's Kiss

True Love's Kiss

Disney Romance
from *Snow White* to *Frozen*

by

Robert Rustad

NEW ELEMENT PUBLISHING

Copyright © 2014 Robert Rustad

All rights reserved. No part of this publication may be reproduced or transmitted in any form or by any means, electronic or mechanical, including photocopy, recording, or any information storage and retrieval system, without permission in writing from the publisher.

Requests for permission to make copies of any part of the work should be submitted by email to:
info@NewElementBooks.com

Published in 2015 by New Element Publishing

ISBN-13 978-1508418511

ISBN-10 1508418519

New Element Publishing
Painted Post, New York
www.NewElementBooks.com

Contents

Introduction

Film has always been my favorite art form. There is something to be said for the spontaneous energy of theatre, or the ability to consume content at one's own pace that comes with the written word, but as far as I'm concerned no storytelling medium surpasses film's complexity or raw power. Other forms of art suggest new worlds of experience, while film conjures them fully. Film is the most complex art form ever devised, taking great resources and labor to complete, and yet this complexity is often obscured from the viewer making it one of the easiest art forms to consume. This gives film a wide appeal, which is a necessity for such an art form.

Because of the need for a wide audience, film has always been a populist medium. This aspect of film is a double-edged sword. Film has the potential to share interesting or even enlightening ideas with an extremely broad audience, but far too many movies fall into the trap of appealing to the lowest common denominator. The power of the filmic illusion is such that all film has the capability of presenting itself as a kind of truth. This holds true even when the film presents an image of the purest fantasy, perhaps even more so, as the unreality of the image before us implicitly denies the reality of our viewing experience. I believe it is of vital importance to study the illusion of film, not to defeat the pleasures of it but to enhance them. To see the aesthetic and narrative aspects of film in detail is to see the painted picture more clearly. This book will serve as an aesthetic and narrative study of film, using one of the most popular and most controversial of all film genres, the Disney Princess film.

Few would deny the extraordinary artistry of Disney's animated catalogue, but beyond that Disney is many things to many people. To some, Walt Disney and the media empire he built is one of the great success stories of American business and cinema. For others, Disney is the staunchest bastion of conservative heteronormativity. Perhaps most controversially, Disney is the steward of American childhood.

Disney's animated films are some of the most popular children's films ever made. The designation of animation as a children's medium is a completely arbitrary one, and thankfully one that is being increasingly challenged in American media, but the fact remains that popular consciousness imagines children as Disney's primary audience and there is a great deal of concern over what messages Disney is presenting to children. Disney has always been a studio built on dreams and wishes. In Disney films, magic is real, good always triumphs, kindness is rewarded, and dreams come true. There is some natural concern that such stories will impart to children the sense that one's desires are sufficient to achieve one's goals, and in the case of girls there is an even greater concern over what those goals should be in the first place. Given Disney's focus on fairy tales, its most recognizable cinematic icons are undoubtedly the Disney Princesses. A great deal of marketing and merchandise is devoted to these characters, and the image that they present to young girls, like that of Barbie dolls, has come under severe scrutiny. The backlash against the Disney Princess franchise is totally justified. Disney marketing presents an image of women whose lives are defined by their good looks and romantic relationships. The backlash against these characters has extended into the films which feature them, and not without good reason. The Disney romance films are filled with many story elements that modern viewers may find troubling. Romances in these films tend to happen quickly, guided by fate or magic rather than any agency of the heroine. A happy marriage is often the great payoff of the film, suggesting the overwhelming importance of romance to the feminine persona. Finally, affairs of the heart are simply that. Impulses and feelings of infatuation are pursued to the fullest, with seemingly rewarding results.

At the time of this writing, Disney's latest film is the astoundingly popular *Frozen*. This film has received an overwhelming amount of praise for challenging the gender and romantic tropes of Disney films. However, there is a certain insidiousness to the self-referential character of this film. The timelessness of Disney films is a testament to both their astounding artistry and their independence from reality, but it comes with the price of homogenization. As each new generation is exposed to the Disney library, their collective image of what Disney is changes. It mixes the oldest with the newest Disney films, and presents a muddled picture of each film by putting it in the same context as films made decades earlier or later. This book will offer criticism of each Disney romance film individually, examining how each differs from the others, with a special focus on each film's gender and romantic aspects. All too often, artistic criticism with a gender focus devolves to little more than accusations of misogyny. This book will undertake an honest analysis of the use of gender and romance in Disney films and the implications of that presentation. Fourteen different films over a period of 76 years are included in order to examine how these factors change over the years. Three essential questions form the basis of this comprehensive analysis. What exactly is the "Disney Romance" genre, how well do recent films like *Frozen* respond to it, and how will it continue to change with the generations?

This book contains analytical arguments, so by default it is an attempt to change opinions. That said, in matters of art, one's opinion matters far less than one's understanding. After reading this book, it is entirely possible that you will not agree with me. All that I hope for is that you will find some new idea in this book, or even just a new way of looking at an idea. I am far less interested in changing opinions than I am in broadening perspectives, which I believe is the most fundamental way in which people grow in their understanding of all things, especially art and entertainment.

Theory

Before a discussion of romantic Disney movies can take place, it is necessary to have some grounding in the general ideas of cinematic romance. A quick discussion of relevant film theory will allow for a deeper dive into the important ideas at the heart of some of Disney's most controversial films. Since this book is about the development of the Disney fairytale romance, this chapter will focus on the ideas of three film theorists in particular. First, we will examine the assumptions and conventions of classic Hollywood romance. Guiding this exploration will be the ideas of Laura Mulvey, one of classical Hollywood's most incisive and insightful critics. The discussion of Mulvey will be supplemented with a summary of the theories of Jacques Lacan. While Lacan is a psychologist more than anything, and his theories do not pertain to film specifically, his ideas have substantial bearing on Mulvey's own theories regarding film as a means of ego identification. Lastly, in order to better understand the process by which *Frozen* eventually resulted from *Snow White and the Seven Dwarfs*, we will briefly touch upon Luis Giannetti's four stages of genre development.

It's no secret that Hollywood has an obsession with romance. If a movie features a man and woman of about the same age, the odds are very good they will be married or dating by the end of the film. In a mystery movie, the detective will fall in love with his client. In a western movie, the marshal will court the rancher's daughter or the local schoolmistress. In a sci-fi movie, the brave space explorer will rescue a captivating alien. A princess who isn't married by the end of her movie is most likely also a pony. Naturally, American cinema has become less saturated with this trope since the golden age of Hollywood (so called by nostalgic film critics, though not wholly without reason) but it is still deeply ingrained in our culture. Even though *Men in Black* presents no evidence that agent J and his new partner have become a couple, many viewers assume that they have.

There is a certain backlash against this storytelling device, but why? Take a look back at the examples provided above—they all involve gender stereotypes of an active male and a passive female. Subversion of this trope has become increasingly common, and this isn't even to say that its use necessarily diminishes the quality of a film. It is, however, worth commenting on a cultural pattern when one is observable, and nobody is more renowned for observation of these particular patterns than Laura Mulvey, who achieved fame with her seminal essay "Visual Pleasure and Narrative Cinema."[1]

Before I present a summary of Mulvey's ideas about Hollywood romance, I should mention that I don't totally agree with them. Her theories rely heavily on Freudian psychological constructs which seem to me sloppy and highly arbitrary compared to more modern theories. Further, her statement of purpose—to do away with narrative film entirely and replace it with avant-garde art films—strikes me as a ludicrous overreaction to the problems with romantic cinema. She reminds me of the Dadaists of the early 20th century, who were so disgusted with the European culture

---

[1] *Screen* 16 (3) 1975: 6-18. doi: 10.1093/screen/16.3.6

which precipitated World War I that they set out on a doomed mission to destroy art and only succeeded in creating a new school of artistic thought. Still, Mulvey has a good eye for both narrative patterns and cinematic techniques, and even if her conclusions and Freudian assumptions seem a bit strange she does do a good job of presenting the essential facts of the situation.

Mulvey's argument is that film provides the audience with two essential pleasures, scopophilia and ego-identification. Scopophilia, the pleasure associated with looking, has obvious ties to voyeurism. People get a certain pleasure from the clandestine observation of others. Sometimes this act can become wound up with a person's sexuality, resulting in invasive voyeuristic behavior, but this overt sexual component is not a necessary part of scopophilia. This pleasure could be as simple as, say, an annoying younger sibling spying on the mundane activities of an older sibling. According to Mulvey, film satisfies this pleasure by giving us a separate world which is totally unaware of the audience. Even though the actors playing the characters know they are being watched, the characters don't and the illusion of film is so convincing that the audience can't help but believe its reality on some level. Mulvey points out that this voyeuristic effect is further enhanced by the darkness of a movie theatre. It's a bit like we're hiding in the shadows while we watch a movie.

The darkness of a movie theater doesn't just create a contrast with the brightness of a movie screen, it also shuts us out from the rest of the audience around us and other visual distractions. This plays into the other great pleasure of cinema, ego-identification. The world that film presents to us is in many ways more appealing than our own. The sets and people all look prettier than what we normally see, the things in the world which are interesting to look at are framed by masterful photographers, the editor helpfully chops up time and space to tell us what is important to look at and when, and the action is usually accompanied by an enchanting musical score. Not only is film aesthetically superior to the real world, but narrative film also seems more structurally appealing in terms of cause and effect. In real life, conflicts are rarely neatly resolved and patterns which might be considered plot threads only occasionally arise. When telling a story, in film or elsewhere, humans apply an order to the universe which is rarely seen in real life. We can't help but be drawn into this beautiful world and so come to identify heavily with our idealized selves, which are reflected in the main characters.

Mulvey connects this phenomenon with nostalgia for the moment where infants recognize their image for what it is and feel a sense of disconnect between their very cute image and the awkward body they inhabit, a stage of psychological development in a model proposed by Jacques Lacan.[2] As a structuralist psychologist, Lacan believes that the human psyche is shaped by the interaction of our core self-awareness with the system of images and languages that comprise our perception of the world. Contact between these two facets of the psyche begins when a baby gains the ability to recognize its own reflection, and a disconnect occurs immediately. The baby's beautiful image does not match the baby's self-perception as an awkward creature unable to communicate its

---

[2] See Lacan, J., "Some Reflections on The Ego" in *International Journal of Psychoanalysis*, 34 (1) 1953: 11–15.

desires or move about easily on its own. This disconnect produces a fascination with the baby's image of itself, a thing which represents it and at the same time is more beautiful than it. An argument could easily be made, however, that such ego-identification is simply a natural result of good storytelling. After all, the audience needs to identify with the characters in any story in order to feel invested in what's going on.

Obviously, there is a great deal of tension between these two pleasures. How are we supposed to clandestinely observe the people in the film world if we're also using them to project ourselves into that world? This is where gender difference enters the situation. The audience is often made to identify with male characters, while women are there for the audience to gaze at. It is from this dichotomy that the idea of a male gaze in cinema arises. The problem isn't simply that most movies don't feature female protagonists, it has more to do with what the female characters contribute to the film. Often times, as recently exemplified in Michael Bay's *Transformers* films, the lead female is totally extraneous to the story. She is there only because the affection of a beautiful woman is a standardized element of the dominant story structure in Hollywood film. By contrast the male lead usually achieves something great and remains active throughout the film, making him seem capable and powerful. When these are the gender roles typical of films, it's understandable that some critics might be concerned with the way female viewers come to perceive their own gender.

It might seem that film has come a long way in the decades since Mulvey wrote this essay. Active female protagonists are indeed increasingly common, particularly in media aimed at children.

But Mulvey's gendered division of labor is far from absent. The scopophilic sexualization of male characters is still very rare and is usually played for comedy. Still, the fact remains that the cultural patterns which Mulvey observed in film are changing.

For a better understanding of how a cinematic genre can develop, let us consult Luis Giannetti's excellent book *Understanding Movies*.[3] Giannetti says that there are four main periods in a genre's development: primitive, classical, revisionist, and parodic. But just what is a genre? Giannetti defines a genre as a set of aesthetic and narrative conventions and values which can be applied to a large body of films. Genres establish a set of expectations in the audience in order to more immediately orient them to their viewing experience, but a film's genre need not be unduly restrictive. Giannetti uses the war genre as an example. A war movie will almost certainly feature some battles and will most likely focus heavily on male characters, but the important particulars of the film vary immensely. What is the film's attitude toward war? Which war does the film focus on? Is the film based on real events? Who are the characters and why should we care that they're in a war?

Giannetti's four stages are organized in terms of the genre's attitude toward its own conventions. At the primitive stage, the genre is still largely a novelty. While many of the genre conventions and values are established, they are not readily recognized as such because the genre has not yet become a part of the popular consciousness and thus hasn't connected with a wide enough

---

[3] *Understanding Movies*, 13th ed. New York: Pearson, 2014. Giannetti's discussion of genre begins on page 354.

audience. One nuance which Giannetti fails to mention is that films retroactively labeled as the primitive stages of their genre are usually considered part of a better established genre when they are created. Universal's 1931 film *Dracula* is often cited as one of the first horror movies, but when it came out it was actually considered a romance film, of all things.[4] *Nosferatu* and *Metropolis* are very different films in terms of tone and setting, but they have enough stylistic similarities and shared historical background that film scholars tend to lump them together into the genre of German Expressionism. There are two points I'm trying to make by injecting this nuance into Giannetti's analysis. One is that which genre a movie is part of is more ambiguous than people might think. The other is that new genres, which are ultimately arbitrary categories of film, are developing all the time, not just during the early years of film.

The second stage of genre development is the classical stage. At this point the genre has gained enough of a popular foothold that its values are recognized and shared by a large portion of the audience. The audience finds the conventions satisfying, guaranteeing an audience for any films marketed as part of this genre. With that guaranteed audience, however, comes a pressure to conform to a certain formula in order to insure their continued satisfaction. This can lead to very simplistic and predictable movies if the formula is adhered to too closely, but this isn't necessarily the case. Consider the 1950s sci-fi film *Forbidden Planet*. The film's story is fairly typical of the time. A group of heroic explorers stumbles

---

[4] See Chapter 1, "Defining Horror," in Peter Hutchings, *The Horror Film*, Harlow, England: Pearson Longman, 2004.

upon a mysterious planet rife with unknown dangers. The main character exposes the stock mad scientist as the unwitting cause of the dangers. Through his heroic actions, the deadly new science is destroyed and the scientist sacrifices himself. Our hero then rockets away from the alien world, taking the scientist's beautiful daughter with him. Based on this simplified synopsis, one might be inclined to dismiss *Forbidden Planet* as trite, but it has several qualities that make it stand out from other space exploration films of the time despite its fairly staid plot.

First of all, the presentation of the film is strikingly underplayed. The score features none of the overblown theremin music which was commonplace in sci-fi at the time. Second, while the film does feature the typical awe and fear of the scientific, it is psychology rather than technology which is the film's primary focus. The former inhabitants of the titular planet achieved technology far beyond anything humanity had achieved even in this hypothetical future which features space exploration, but their failure to keep the darker side of their psyches in check led to the accidental creation of psychically projected monsters which consumed the whole race. This might seem like the most hokey of pop psychology to the modern viewer, but it really was a conspicuous departure from the atomophobia which was the default concern of 50s sci-fi. In fact, a strong case could be made that *Forbidden Planet* was the main precursor to *Star Trek*, one of science fiction's definitive franchises. A major theme of *Star Trek* is the exploration of the human frailties which will still exist even after humans have learned to live in accord with their technology. In short, just because a film uses many of the narrative conventions of its genre doesn't mean that it lacks aesthetic or intellectual value to its audience.

In the revisionist stage, the conventions of the genre are reexamined and often heavily modified. Revisionist films tend to be more morally ambiguous and seldom feature a happy ending or a morally satisfying resolution to a tragedy. Giannetti characterizes the revisionist film as more intellectually than emotionally satisfying. Here is the point where one begins to see the greatest flaw in Giannetti's criticism, his privileging of his own era's narrative vogue. Despite his defense of film genres as a general concept, he dismisses straightforward adherence to their conventions as infantile and naive. He makes the mistake of believing that because moral ambiguity and irony are the most popular attitudes of storytelling at this point in time, every style of storytelling which came before was somehow less sophisticated.

Giannetti's sequential idea of genre development is also problematic because of the great overlap which exists between the classical and revisionist stages. He offers the Clint Eastwood western *Unforgiven* as an example of revisionist film. *Unforgiven* takes Eastwood out of his element as a merciless yet justified anti-hero, and puts him in the role of a retired gunman filled with regret. He grimly philosophizes about the realities of violence and death, rather than just smiling before them as much younger Eastwood characters did in the spaghetti westerns of the 1960s and 1970s. While the grim-faced, fearless gunslinger who can shoot his way out of any situation without compunction fits perfectly with many viewers' idea of the classic western hero, it's important to remember that at the time the spaghetti westerns were made they were considered a drastic departure from the conventions of Hollywood westerns from the 1940s and 1950s. The heroes changed from white-hatted pillars of law and order to self-serving magnificent bastards with hearts of gold. They wouldn't hesitate to fight dirty, they were often criminals, and anyone they killed bled. Again, we see how a film's position within its genre is subject to change. Today's revisionist film is tomorrow's classical film. We see the idealized westerns and war films of the 1950s as products of runaway nationalist fervor combined with a touch of paranoia regarding the spread of communism and a need to legitimize our national narrative. Who is to say that future generations will not look with equal bemusement upon brilliant modern revisionist films like *The Dark Night* as the product of a time and place plagued by rapid technological change coupled with crippling distrust and fear of a world which has suddenly become much more interconnected?

The final stage of genre development is the parodic stage. Here, the conventions of the genre are largely adhered to, but also mocked. While this stage seems fairly self-explanatory, it should be noted that the best parodic films offer an insightful critique of their source material. A prime example of film parody is Mel Brooks' *Spaceballs*. Many classic sci-fi conventions are mocked in this film, especially those found in *Star Wars*. The film features a comically large spaceship that references the great size of a star destroyer, interprets the typical space explorer as a vagabond in a Winnebago, and even transforms the wise and spiritually inclined Yoda into a wisecracking alien obsessed with merchandising the very film he appears in.

The overarching problem with Giannetti's film genre analysis it is that it is only functional for a certain time period. While Giannetti acknowledges that the development of a film genre is not absolutely sequential (that is to say, films with a classical genre sensibility can certainly be made after the genre has reached the revisionist stage) the organization of the different stages makes it clear that he only considers the state of a genre at any time relative to what it is now, and fails to consider genre films in their original context. That said, he presents a model of genre development that makes logical sense and provokes the consideration of a film's relationship to a larger genre construct. More importantly, he exposes the complexity and variety present in film genres. While the construct of film genres is completely arbitrary in the abstract, Giannetti at least sheds some light on persistent developmental patterns within that construct.

What do these theories have to do with Disney movies? The last half of Mulvey's essay revolves around a Freudian analysis of female guilt in film which may not be especially applicable to the Disney heroines (with one exception that will be touched on in a later chapter), but her analysis of female passivity and the gendered division of labor with regard to audience pleasure is relevant to all film. Disney films are a slight anomaly with regard to cinematic gender roles in that female protagonists have always been fairly common in them, especially in those modeled after fairy tales, but the stereotype still exists of a passive princess who waits to be rescued or for wishes to come true. While there are many exceptions (indeed I will argue that straightforward adherence to this trope is the exception) this paradigm colors the entire Disney image. When examining how closely a Disney heroine adheres to the gender expectations of the dominant cinematic ideology, three essential questions must be asked: To what extent is the audience enabled to identify with the character? To what extent is the character endowed with agency and autonomy? What is the character's relationship to the other characters in the film? These three questions combine to address the larger question at the heart of feminist film criticism: Does the film offer a positive, or at least healthy, portrayal of women to the public? This question is particularly relevant to Disney films because of the often very young age of the viewers.

As for Giannetti, while his views on genre development might be somewhat limited to the here and now, they are useful for understanding that a category of film does change over time. One peculiar phenomenon of Disney films is their timeless quality. Children today are just as likely to enjoy a Disney film as those who were children when it was made. As each new generation is exposed to the entirety of the Disney animated catalogue, the films tend to be misleadingly conflated as part of a larger "Disney Image." It is important to remember, however, that these films have been made over a very long period of time, and that their historical contexts are reflected in the films themselves. Styles of storytelling and artistry evolve over the decades. In this book, we will see how Disney films grow based on what came before, and hopefully gain an appreciation for the radical transformation of the fairytale narrative which resulted in *Frozen*.

Each one of the films discussed in this book has its own relationship to the traditional Disney conventions, and each has its own narrative considerations. These will be addressed in the coming chapters, but consider this chapter a theoretical touchstone for the entire book. To a greater or lesser degree, varying from movie to movie, the issues of the film's relationship to the classical Disney narrative and its treatment of its heroines will be addressed.

The chapters ahead will cover every animated Disney film which features as a key plot point a romance between two human characters, and which is not a sequel to another film. No animal romances, such as those in *Lady and the Tramp* or *The Lion King*, will be covered because it makes little sense to apply human standards to relationships between animals, even anthropomorphized ones. This book will also cover the mostly live-action comedy *Enchanted*, since it provides direct commentary on Disney romantic tropes. Special attention will be paid to films featuring Disney's most marketed characters, the Disney Princesses. *Brave*, which features Princess Merida, will not be covered since it does not have a romantic relationship to critique and is not made by Disney Animation Studios.

No sequel films will be covered because, in addition to Disney sequels rarely being of very high quality, any romantic relationships featured in them are usually rehashes of romances from the original film or they are constrained by the parameters of that romance in some way rather than building off the Disney canon as a whole. The primary purpose of this book is to serve as a critical reexamination of films which have influenced the sensibilities and expectations of many children, so it makes little sense to devote chapters to films which audiences have largely (and rightfully) forgotten.

Snow White and the Seven Dwarfs

Snow White and the Seven Dwarfs is the first full length animated film in cinematic history, and this fact alone assures Walt Disney's place in the popular culture as one of the great innovators of film. The transition from seven minute comical cartoons to a project running more than ten times that length is reflected in the simplicity of the film's story. A princess named Snow White grows up working as a scullery maid under the rule of her stepmother, the unnamed evil Queen. The Queen's ego is threatened by Snow White's beauty when her magic mirror proclaims the Princess as the fairest in the land. One day, as Snow White wishes out loud to find love, a prince arrives at the castle and admiringly serenades her. That same day, the Queen sends a hunter in her employ to take Snow White into the forest and kill her. The hunter tries to follow orders, but his fondness for her breaks his murderous resolve at the last second. Asking for forgiveness, he informs Snow White of the Queen's intent and tells her to run away and hide.

Snow White flees into the forest in a panic, eventually calming down enough to assess the situation and look for a place to stay. With the help of some friendly animals, she finds a small house and cleans it up in hopes that the inhabitants will allow her to stay in exchange. After cleaning the house and setting a pot of stew to boil, Snow White retires to the house's bedroom, taking note of the names on the little beds she supposes belong to orphaned children. Meanwhile, the dwarfs who own the cottage return home from a day of working in the mines to find the house cleaned. After much speculation about some monstrous influence, they go upstairs to find Snow White. With the exception of a dwarf named Grumpy, the group takes to her easily and agrees to shelter her. As Snow White passes the evening singing, dancing, and teaching the dwarfs hygienic discipline, the Queen finds out that Snow White is alive by consulting her mirror. She proceeds to magically disguise herself as an aged apple peddler in order to give Snow White a poisonous apple which will cause the victim to appear dead until the reception of love's first kiss (subtly but importantly distinct from the idea of true love's kiss).

The next day, while the dwarfs are off working, the Queen visits the cottage and tells Snow White that the apple she offers her is magical and will make wishes come true upon being bitten. At the same time, the animals who accompanied Snow White to the cottage recognize the Queen. Failing to drive her away from the cottage, they rush to the dwarfs for assistance. By the time the dwarfs return, Snow White has bitten the apple and fallen unconscious. The Queen is pursued to the top of a rocky precipice, and prepares to send a boulder tumbling down on the dwarfs. Just then, she is struck by a bolt of lightning and begins a long tradition of Disney villains falling to their deaths. The dwarfs mourn Snow White and build her a glass coffin. A long time afterward, most likely months but possibly years, the Prince comes and kisses Snow White. She is revived and the two ride off together amid much jubilation from the dwarfs and animals.

Upon viewing the film, the heavily lopsided nature of its narrative becomes clear. The Prince, who provides the resolution to the story as well as the basis for Snow White's aspirations, appears only in the first and last of the scenes with Snow White. Where he has been for the whole film, and why he left the woman he apparently loved so much is never explained—for that matter, neither is his role in this world's power structure. Is he the Prince of a neighboring kingdom, or a subject of the Queen? Not even his name is revealed. Putting aside the completely superfluous Prince for a moment, the film also has characters like the huntsman who are introduced once to move the plot forward and never brought up again. Further, the great majority of the film's runtime is dedicated to the one night that the dwarfs spend with Snow White, which has little to do with the ostensible conflict in the end. Finally, the issue of Snow White's seeming death is resolved in mere minutes of screen time, almost as soon as it is introduced. Such a resolution seems poor dramatic payoff for the suspenseful parallel editing between the sinister hag and the frantic dwarfs that builds up to her eating the apple.

Despite these seeming flaws, it would be misleading to describe *Snow White and the Seven Dwarfs* as poorly plotted. It would be more accurate to say that the film foregoes an emphasis on plot in favor of novelty and striking visuals. Such a statement may seem like an after-the-fact rationalization for poor storytelling, but it is totally consistent with the film's original context. Hindsight reveals that *Snow White and the Seven Dwarfs* began the expansion of cartoons into more traditionally cinematic films, but a comparison of the film to other animated entertainment of the era makes it clear that this was not the film's intent. Rather than applying the conventions of cinema to a cartoon, the film seems more like an attempt to make a cartoon an entertainment event equal to mainstream cinema. The film shares many of the same conventions as contemporary Disney shorts, including a heavy emphasis on music. Consider the songs the dwarfs sing. "Heigh Ho" is of course the most famous, but they also sing a song when washing up for dinner and another while relaxing with Snow White. In all three cases, the songs have very little to do with the development of plot threads or character arcs. They are catchy songs that provide an opportunity for humorous animation, rather like the Silly Symphony cartoons produced by Disney at the time. This isn't to say that such cartoons had no plots to speak of, but as in *Snow White and the Seven Dwarfs* the plots were told in very broad strokes. Take as an example the short cartoon *The Goddess of Spring*, in which the Greek story of Persephone's capture and seasonal return from the Underworld is retold in a simplified form. On paper, the plot's emphasis is on the dynamic between the Goddess and her devilish kidnapper. Yet the cartoon puts most of its focus on the musical capering of the Goddess' friends and the Devil's minions.

Modern audiences might be inclined to dismiss *Snow White*'s ostensibly poor plotting as a symptom of the film's age, but a cursory knowledge of mainstream films in the late 1930s and even earlier in the history of cinema reveals that screenwriters have made use of intricate plots almost from the beginning of film itself. Finally, pushing the boundaries of animation is consistent with other Disney films made shortly after *Snow White*. Disney's third film, *Fantasia*, is also an attempt to expand the idea of what a cartoon is capable of. *Fantasia* is an anthology of animated segments that more or less share the length of a standard animated short, but use classic orchestral music rather than popular ditties as a basis for the animation. All of this suggests that even as Disney attempted to experiment with removing the self-imposed limits of animation, it was still viewed as a medium distinct from mainstream film. This uniqueness serves *Snow White* well. Unlike many primitive examples of film genres, *Snow White* didn't originate as part of a different genre construct. It isn't like any other film because it isn't trying to be a film at all, but a very long and very beautiful cartoon. Thus, it establishes a distinct identity for itself and for Disney's animated cinema from the outset.

Viewed in this light, the film's bare-bones romance makes perfect sense. Whenever romance occurs in musical cartoon shorts, it must be established in just a few seconds in order to allow the majority of the cartoon to be devoted to comic mischief, usually the conflict between the protagonist and a villain who pursues the female lead (either literally or figuratively, or even both). The romance seen in *Snow White* may seem farfetched, but it is a natural outgrowth of the conventions of the Silly Symphony rather than a malicious attempt to oversimplify romance in the minds of young girls. This isn't to say that the Disney Princess marketing franchise doesn't exploit the film to that effect—even *Mulan* is not immune from such exploitation.

Snow White's gender politics are a very mixed bag. In ways, the film is remarkably progressive for its time. It also buys heavily into retrograde assumptions and sets unfortunate narrative precedent, particularly where its villain is concerned. The villainess is motivated purely by her jealousy of another's physical beauty, but at least she is obsessed with her beauty for its own sake. She isn't dependent on a man for validation. One could argue that the masculine figure in her magic mirror counts as a source of male validation, but the mirror could also represent the Queen's self-image and self-absorption. That possibility, however, serves to highlight the most problematic aspect of the Queen's character. She is an unabashed indictment of feminine power.

If the slave in the mirror represents the Queen's self-image, one might read the situation thusly: The Queen is not dependent on male validation because she considers her power equal to that of a male. This is also reflected in the film's art design. The Queen's throne is decorated to look like a peacock. This is obviously a reference to the Queen's vanity, but it also carries with it masculine coding, since it is male peacocks who have ostentatious plumage. The Queen is described as being vain and jealous, and though these failings exist primarily in relation to Snow White's beauty, it would be understandable to conclude that they extend to the Queen's relationship to masculine power, and that her audacity in wielding that power is the source of her corruption. Whether these problematic implications are intentional or not, they continue to be a vital part of the evil Queen archetype today.

Snow White herself might seem like a poor role model to modern audiences. Her great coming-of-age achievement is to keep house for a group of men who are also metaphors for children and teach them to wash themselves. Such concerns regarding the image of womanhood *Snow White* presents to young girls are valid, particularly since young audiences simply will not have the historical context to understand that motherhood as the truest expression of womanhood is an archaic idea. However, to write Snow White off as an attempt to keep women in the home ignores the original context of the film.

In 1937, homemaking was the primary occupation for many American women and yet it was hardly ever the primary activity of a protagonist in a film. *Snow White and the Seven Dwarfs* might not have challenged patriarchal assumptions about the role of women, but it did attempt to give women a protagonist they could identify with. This is a drastic change from the standard gendered division of labor described in the last chapter. Not only is Snow White the film's protagonist, but aside from the mention of her beauty and a couple of intimate close ups she is hardly sexualized at all. Further, even if most modern mothers also have jobs outside the home, motherhood remains an important part of many women's lives, making Snow White a very relatable character still. Perhaps one day of washing and cooking for some dwarfs doesn't capture the real difficulty and commitment that motherhood represents, but it is after all just a metaphor.

Disney promotional material often refers to *Snow White and the Seven Dwarfs* as "the one that started it all." To a certain extent this is true. This film began the image of the dainty Disney Princess romance, established the association between Disney films and music, and cemented Disney as the forerunner in animation. Still, most of what *Snow White* started builds upon what came before, and the conventions it established have evolved through the decades to become more and more like what the audience expects from a feature film. *Snow White and the Seven Dwarfs* may have been the beginning of Disney in many important ways, but this book will show that it is not even close to the end.

Cinderella

Cinderella marks the first Disney film since *Snow White and the Seven Dwarfs* (10 films earlier) to retell a fairy tale, and the first one since *Bambi* (six films earlier) to tell a single story instead of utilizing an anthology format. Much like Snow White, Cinderella is beleaguered by a wicked stepmother who forces her into the role of servant in her own home. Despite this, Cinderella maintains an upbeat attitude and dreams of a better future. She suffers cruelly at the hands of her stepfamily, but shows great kindness to the mice and birds that live in the attic of her family's chateau with her. One day, when the Prince of this imaginary kingdom is soon to return from a non-specific absence, the King decides to hold a ball in order to help his son choose a wife, since he is impatient to become a grandfather. Cinderella's family receives an invitation, and the stepmother gives Cinderella many extra chores to ensure she will be unable to attend. Cinderella's chores do indeed keep her busy all day, but her mouse friends surprise her with her mother's old dress augmented with accessories discarded by her stepsisters. Unaware of the accessories' origins, Cinderella attempts to join her family as they leave for the ball, only to have her stepsisters tear her dress apart as retribution for her supposed theft.

Heartbroken, Cinderella retreats to the garden and laments of ever achieving happiness. Before Cinderella can fall into complete despair, her fairy godmother arrives and uses magic to give her a carriage and a new dress. She goes to the ball and dances with a young man, unaware that he is the Prince. The two fall in love, but Cinderella has to run away from the castle before the fairy godmother's spell wears off and her dress and carriage revert to rags and a pumpkin. As she flees, she leaves behind a glass slipper, but keeps the other one. The King, anxious for his son to be married, sends his Grand Duke to search for the young woman. The stepmother hears about the search and discovers that Cinderella is the woman in question based on her humming a tune played at the ball. She locks Cinderella upstairs in preparation for the Grand Duke's arrival, but Cinderella is able to escape just in time with the help of the mice and the family dog. The stepmother maliciously breaks the glass slipper by tripping the duke, but Cinderella proves her identity by producing the other one. Thus, she and the Prince are married.

Cinderella marks both the beginning of the classical phase of the Disney Princess genre and the true introduction of the Disney Princess to mainstream film. The film has many similarities to *Snow White and the Seven Dwarfs*. In addition to the basic premise of the upbeat servant girl and the wicked stepmother, much of the film is spent following the antics of the comical side characters. However, these elements are tied together better to make a tighter script. For example, the mice are usually doing something directly related to Cinderella herself. They make Cinderella's dress, serve as her horses, and help her escape the attic by stealing the key from the stepmother. Even the seemingly unrelated things they do help to explore Cinderella's character.

In the opening sequence of the film, a mouse named Gus fails to obtain any leftover corn when Cinderella feeds the chateau's chickens, giving her the opportunity to show kindness by giving him a stack of kernels. More importantly, Gus hides from the family cat Lucifer in the cup on one of the stepsister's breakfast plates. The scene of Lucifer trying to figure out which cup contains the mouse is suspenseful and entertaining in its own right, but when Gus is discovered by the stepsister it provides the first look at the dynamic between Cinderella and her family. There is a great contrast in how she is treated by her stepsisters and stepmother. The sisters are mean, but their meanness lacks sophistication. They shout at Cinderella and insult her, but Cinderella is able to shrug their cruelty off most of the time because she knows how petty they are. The stepmother, on the other hand, is controlled and stern. She doesn't insult Cinderella, and she actually puts on a genteel but ominous façade most of the time. She only raises her voice if Cinderella talks out of turn.

One point of interest with the stepmother is that while she consistently favors her daughters over Cinderella, she extends some of her nasty and controlling parenting to them as well. The one thing that consistently silences the sisters' bickering is a softly spoken command from their mother, and she even tells them that when the Grand Duke comes searching for the woman who fits the slipper she will consider having the wrong shoe size a failure on their part. It is possible that she views her daughters as failures to some degree already. After all, it was her overindulgence of them that led the chateau she had married into to lose its prestige. The only everyday activity we see her undertake is instructing her daughters in a music lesson, a refined activity sure to make them appealing to the nobility. In a strange way, the stepmother has dug herself into a very deep hole. She's squandered her prestige spoiling her daughters, who are now her only chance to regain it. Unfortunately, being both ugly and spoiled, they are not appealing to any prestigious bachelors. The only really eligible member of the household, Cinderella, has been treated so cruelly by her guardian that she would never help her if she were to marry a nobleman, so power over Cinderella is the only power the stepmother is likely to ever obtain again.

Here again we see a woman corrupted by power which is rightfully masculine, having usurped control of the chateau from Cinderella's kind father. In this film, however, the problematic implications are somewhat mitigated by the fact that the step mother's obsessions are prestige and control (she is admittedly stated to be jealous of Cinderella, but her actions largely appear motivated more by a need for control). These obsessions carry decidedly gender-neutral cultural codes, as opposed to the feminine coding in the evil Queen's obsession with beauty. In addition, while Cinderella's father is held up as a paragon of male authority, the King is shown to be impulsive and buffoonish to the point of incompetence.

The increased detail of the relationships between these characters is yet another way in which *Cinderella* is more similar to a mainstream film. In *Snow White and the Seven Dwarfs*, Snow White and the Queen are never seen to interact except when the Queen is disguised as a peddler. No clear sense of Snow White's life in the castle is given. Cinderella is also given a more concrete backstory. Snow White's was given on a couple pages of illuminated introductory text, but Cinderella's is told with full visuals and narration. This detailed characterization extends to the film's romance as well. Cinderella and the Prince don't have any more romantic motivation than Snow White and her Prince did, but at least in *Cinderella* the King is seen discussing his plans for his son to be married. To the film's credit, it is well aware of how ludicrous this fairytale romance is. Just before the Prince meets Cinderella, the Grand Duke proceeds to narrate the King's imagined sequence of events in jest, saying that such a thing can only happen in fantasy. In an earlier scene, the King illustrates his plan by kicking philosophy books out from between two book ends which look like a man and a woman, symbolically abandoning rationalism to further the fairytale story.

Such touches of self-awareness lend the film a certain grounding in reality in spite of its constant use of fantasy. The film is also more grounded in reality by the characters' use of language. *Snow White and the Seven Dwarfs* takes place in a highly nebulous storybook land. If it has any connection with the real world it is in the anachronistic prospector mannerisms of the dwarf Grumpy. By contrast, the characters in *Cinderella* use words like "chateau," "mademoiselle" and "senora." The film's visual style is also less like a story-book. *Snow White* made highly dramatic use of light and shadow, but the lighting in *Cinderella* is mostly flat except for occasional low key lighting to accentuate the stepmother's nastiness. The backgrounds also seem less like the bucolic vison one might have of a medieval forest and more like an ornamental renaissance town. Even the dress of the male nobles is more analogous to real life. They look more like Napoleonic nobles than stereotypical medieval ones. The wardrobes of the women in the film also lend to this sense of temporal nebulosity. The mice are seen constructing Cinderella's dress with the help of a tape measure, a device that did not exist until the 20th century. There is a tension in the film's aesthetic between the modern and the pseudohistorical, which gives the film a unique look and feel.

Even though *Cinderella* has more of a plot than *Snow White* in general, it still doesn't have very compelling main characters. Cinderella has even less direction and personality than Snow White. At least Snow White has a goal, to not be killed by her stepmother. Cinderella has goals as well, but the audience is never told what they are. In fact, Cinderella makes it a point not to reveal her dreams to anyone for fear they won't come true. She doesn't start out wanting to marry the Prince. She doesn't even know the Prince when she sees him at the ball. Even after she falls in love with him, she doesn't expect to see him again after running from the castle and she seems largely content all the same. She does want to go to the ball, but she doesn't know about it when the film starts and it's just an example of something she can do other than stay home and do chores. The Prince is even less developed. Like the Prince from *Snow White and the Seven Dwarfs*, he has only a few lines of dialogue. The audience gets incomplete information about his life as well. We are told he's returning to the kingdom, but where was he? Was it a war? A diplomatic mission? A vacation? A pilgrimage? Still, at least the audience gets the sense that he has a life outside of the film.

Even though the main characters are largely bereft of life and personality in favor of the much more dynamic side characters, Cinderella is still a largely positive role model. She doesn't allow herself to become bitter and makes the best of a bad situation. Despite all the thematic emphasis that the film puts on her dreams, she is a very active character. She doesn't just put up with the abuse of her stepfamily, but finds small ways of defying them. She stands up to her stepmother and insists upon her right to attend the ball. She shelters mice that her family wouldn't think twice about feeding to Lucifer. She even refuses to do the bidding of her stepsisters once she hears that the Grand Duke is coming to the chateau. Her dreams themselves are a form of defiance. Cinderella says at one point that her desires and sense of self are the one aspect of her life that no one else can control.

Admittedly, Cinderella isn't able to overcome her situation by herself. She needs the mice to rescue her, she needs her fairy godmother to get her into the ball, and she needs the Prince to marry her. Still, these actions are rewards for the virtues that Cinderella exhibits. The mice rescue her to repay her kindness, her fairy godmother rewards her optimism, and the Prince is a reward for her perseverance. The Prince is perhaps the most surprising reward for Cinderella. In classical Hollywood films, it is almost always the woman who is the reward for the man's actions and virtues.

Cinderella is not the most coherent or focused of the Disney Princess films, owing perhaps to the studio's long hiatus from standard feature filmmaking. Still, it presents a positive vision of hard work and kindness rewarded and some very enjoyable side characters. Disney's side characters steal the show in both *Snow White and The Seven Dwarfs* and *Cinderella*, and they will continue to be the most interesting part of the next Princess film, which is in many ways is the culmination of the narrative formula laid out in the earlier Disney canon.

Sleeping Beauty

Sleeping Beauty was the last Disney Princess film to be produced before the period known as the Disney Renaissance. The film tells the story of a young Princess named Aurora, whose birth is celebrated by all the subjects of a 14th century kingdom. Three good fairies, Flora, Fauna and Merriweather, attend the celebration to bestow upon the infant supernatural gifts of great beauty and musical affinity. Before the final gift can be granted, an immortal evil creature (possibly a fairy herself) named Maleficent appears and curses Aurora to die by touching a spinning wheel before sunset on her 16th birthday. Merriweather weakens the curse so that Aurora will not die, but instead fall asleep and be revived by true love's kiss. As an added precaution, the fairies take Aurora into the forest to raise her in secret.

For the next 16 years, Maleficent's minions fail to locate the Princess. Their failure is partly due to the fairies concealing themselves by foregoing the use of magic and partly due to the minions' assumption that Aurora has remained a baby all these years. On Aurora's 16th birthday, the fairies send her out to pick some berries while they prepare a birthday party for her. While in the forest, Aurora (who believes her name to be Briar Rose) laments the lonely life she leads with her supposed aunts and speaks to the forest animals of the handsome prince she often sees in her dreams. Her singing voice draws the attention of a young man riding in the forest. The pair sing, dance and fall in love. Before either party can exchange identities, Aurora hurries back to her home and tells the young man to follow her there later that evening. Unbeknownst to Aurora, she is already betrothed to the young man. His name is Prince Phillip (the first of the Disney Princes to have a name), and his father King Hubert made an arrangement with King Stefan (Aurora's father) at the Princess' birth to have their children married.

The fairies, unable to properly make a dress or cake for the Princess, resort to using magic. The signs of this activity are observed by Maleficent's pet crow, who stays and watches long enough for Aurora to come home and for her true identity to be revealed. The conversation which follows also reveals that Aurora is to be taken back to Stefan's castle that night, and that the young man she fell in love with will come to the cottage that night.

Forced to leave the cottage and her new love, Aurora is taken to the castle in a state of great sadness. The fairies secretly bring her into the castle, and leave her alone with her grief for a moment. During this time, Maleficent appears in the form of a glowing green light and lures Aurora to a secret chamber where she touches the prophesied spinning wheel and falls asleep just before sunset. When the fairies return and lament their failure to protect Aurora, they decide to put the whole kingdom to sleep in order to spare them any heartbreak. Just before King Hubert falls asleep, he drowsily reveals to Flora that the young man Aurora fell in love with is indeed Phillip.

The fairies rush back to the cottage to intercept him, only to find that he has been captured by Maleficent and taken to her castle. Recognizing that Phillip can undo her spell with true love's kiss, she plans to keep him locked in her dungeon for 100 years before allowing him to leave and revive Aurora. The fairies free Phillip and assist him in fighting his way out of Maleficent's castle. Furious, Maleficent attempts to stop him, first by sending magic lightning bolts which he dodges, then with a wall of thorns around Stefan's castle which he cuts his way though. Finally she flies to the castle herself and transforms into a fire-breathing dragon. After killing Maleficent in a pitched battle, Phillip enters the castle and revives Aurora. The fairies' spell over the rest of the kingdom fades and the Prince and Princess live happily ever after.

The most striking thing about *Sleeping Beauty* is the scope of the story. The film takes place on a far grander scale than had ever been attempted by Disney before. *Snow White and the Seven Dwarfs* and *Cinderella* are dramatic enough stories, to be sure, but they focus only on the trials and fortunes of a few people and the conflicts are resolved in a matter of days. *Sleeping Beauty* tells a story which takes place over the course of 16 years, and the fate of an entire kingdom is bound up with the resolution. On top of that, *Sleeping Beauty* continues the trend set by *Cinderella* of increasingly fleshing out the fantasy world in which it takes place. In *Cinderella*, details like royal decrees and noble titles were introduced. In *Sleeping Beauty*, the power structure of the kingdom and such ideas as diplomatic marriage are explored in great detail. In fact, an entire musical number is devoted to a diplomatic conversation between Stefan and Hubert. The more fantastic elements of the setting are likewise much more detailed than in previous films. Unlike in *Cinderella*, magic isn't just introduced to provide an instant solution to a problem. The fairies who hide Aurora have to work around the limitations of their magic, and they and Maleficent have very distinct domains of magic that both parties must use their cleverness to contend with at times, as opposed to raw power. For example, the magical sword that kills Maleficent is created by the fairies, but they themselves are not able to use it. They depend on Phillip to kill Maleficent for them because his love transforms violence into something positive. The problematic implications of this situation will be explored later in this chapter, but it shows a further shift in Disney films toward a more specific and well-plotted narrative.

Prince Phillip himself is an example of this film's increased emphasis on character. Phillip might not be very interesting when compared with future Disney male leads such as Aladdin or the Beast, but his actions contribute to the story and he has conversations with his horse and his father and not just Aurora. The film even dares to put him in humorous situations, such as the scene where he falls off his horse and into a forest stream. Unfortunately, the same valor and heroism that make Phillip easily the most engaging of the early Disney Princes also establishes him as the archetype of the stereotypical Disney Prince. All he seems to do is fight and pursue beautiful women. What's worse, he earns the affections of the woman in question through combat alone. Yes, he does have the self-assurance to stand up to his father about his intentions to marry an unknown woman, but to abdicate his birthright and throw the kingdom into chaos for a romantic whim speaks to a deep predilection for irresponsibility.

Phillip's existence as a masculine stereotype is surely not helped by his juxtaposition with Aurora. It is difficult to imagine a character more passive than Aurora. Throughout the film she literally makes no choices or takes any action of her own. She goes out picking berries because the fairies tell her to. She falls in love with Phillip because he's the first man she sees and he is similar to a romantic figure of her dreams. She touches the spinning wheel not by any choice of her own, but because she is enchanted by Maleficent. Aurora's only purpose in this film is to serve as an object of desire for Phillip and an object of hatred for Maleficent. She is the ultimate example of the gendered division of labor posited by Laura Mulvey. Her only characteristics are her physical beauty and her talent for song. Her only desire is for male appreciation. The Princesses before her have romances which are just as shallow, but they manage to be positive characters in their own right. They have their own virtues and their own ambitions. Aurora has nothing but shallow dreams, all of which come true, and none of which she earns.

Disney films of the period seem to have a consistent fascination with dreams. *Cinderella* places a great deal of importance of having faith in one's dreams, for example. This fascination extends beyond fairy tales. *Alice in Wonderland*'s story is revealed at the end to have been the main character's dream, and *Peter Pan* blurs the line between dreams and its own reality. At times Peter appears to be present in the physical world, and Mr. Darling appears to recognize the ship-shaped cloud that sails through the sky in the ending scene. Yet the film ends with Wendy waking up and her parents coming back from a party that same night despite all the time that passed in Neverland. Even earlier films share an affinity for dreams, but their focus is less on literal dreaming characters and instead on highly abstract and surreal interludes. Dumbo's drunken visions of pink elephants and the less narrative segments of *Fantasia* are fine examples. *Sleeping Beauty* melds together all of the dream related tropes from prior films. When Aurora receives her gifts from the fairies, a series of highly stylized colors and shapes representative of stars and birds swirl about the frame accompanied by a choral lullaby. The film also includes the narrative blending of dreams and reality. Aurora falls in love with Phillip after seeing him just once in real life, but she has apparently had many dreams beforehand in which she shared long talks with someone broadly similar to him. Given that magic and prophecy are accepted facts of this fantasy world, it is entirely possible that Aurora and Phillip actually have shared some kind of magical dream experience due to their betrothal. Not that such a possibility would excuse their poor character development. If they have literally met through their dreams, some representation of these encounters would be appreciated.

The focus of early Disney films on dreams is often criticized. It is seen as an encouragement of dreams over action. In the case of *Sleeping Beauty*, perhaps such a concern is justified. While the fairies are shown to be selfless and courageous, and given a great deal of respect despite their lack of conventional beauty, the film's romantic leads simply fall into each other's arms and have happiness handed to them. Still *Sleeping Beauty* is more than redeemable if one considers the film itself as one would a dream. Despite the increased detail given to the story and to side characters, the film sets itself up as more of a cinematic and musical experience than a didactic story. The art style of the film presents a flat and angular world far removed from *Snow White and the Seven Dwarfs'* early attempt at photorealism in its human characters. That and the intense focus on immortal and elementally moral characters makes the story seem far removed from human endeavor. Still, the question remains of whether the crafting of beautiful dreams is a transcendent cinematic experience or an emotionally crippling opiate.

Whatever the case, this film marks the last time for decades that Disney films would return to the study of fairy tales and princesses, and with this film as the most sophisticated in that category the Ur-example of a dreaming passive princess and a shallow instant romance was set. After a long interim however, the next two romance-focused Disney films would see to the disposition of these tropes. The next film discussed will show a princess just as desire-driven and just as shallow, but with a personality to compensate. The film to follow that will unveil a well-developed romance and provide Disney's subtlest and most sincere critique of its own formula.

The Little Mermaid

The Little Mermaid marks the return of Disney to fairytale romance after a hiatus of three decades, and the beginning of the Disney Renaissance. The implication of that phrase, which was coined retroactively, is that the Princess romances are the films which are most essential to the studio's identity. If the term "Disney Renaissance" were coined by the studio itself, one might suspect that it was making an active effort to homogenize its product in order to cement its corporate image, brushing aside some of its most subdued and clever films as an awkward departure from coming of age fantasy stories.

The film's main character is Ariel, a 16-year-old mermaid princess possessed of a fascination with all things relating to humanity. When she misses an engagement to sing in a concert arranged for her father King Triton to investigate a sunken ship for human artifacts, Triton instructs a crab named Sebastian to follow Ariel and make sure she doesn't go to the surface of the ocean. Sebastian finds Ariel in a secret grotto where she has secreted away a collection of human objects. As he speaks with Ariel, a ship passes overhead. Ariel investigates the vessel to find that a party is being held aboard in honor of a human prince named Eric. Ariel watches the party in secret, and falls in love with Eric. A statue of the Prince is unveiled by his butler Grimsby, who urges Eric to find a wife. Soon afterward, a storm threatens the ship. Most of the sailors are able to evacuate, but Eric is blown overboard by an exploding barrel of gunpowder. Ariel saves Eric from drowning, and sings to him as he regains consciousness. She hears Grimsby rushing onto the beach where she took Eric, and retreats. Confused by his ordeal, Eric has no idea that Ariel is a mermaid, nor even a clear idea of what her face looks like. The only way he can recognize her is by her singing voice. Eric has fallen in love with her and resolves to find her. Ariel, meanwhile, becomes more infatuated with Eric, to the point where it becomes clear to everyone around her that she is in love. Triton is intent on discovering the identity of Ariel's love and summons Sebastian, who lets slip that Ariel has fallen in love with a human.

As Ariel admires the statue of Eric that her fish friend Flounder somehow recovered, Triton follows Sebastian to Ariel's grotto and confronts her. When Ariel insists that she loves Eric, Triton destroys her collection in a fit of pique. Her anger and sorrow clouding her judgment, Ariel is persuaded by a pair of sinister eels to seek help from a sea witch named Ursula, an obese octopus woman who was banished from Triton's palace for unspecified reasons. Ursula has a scheme to take revenge on Triton and take his kingdom for herself. Using Ariel as an unwitting pawn, she offers to make her a human in exchange for her voice. Once on the surface, she will have three days to win Eric's love and receive true love's kiss from him. Should she fail, she will return to the sea as the property of Ursula.

Sebastian tries and fails to counsel Ariel against such a deal. After the transformation, he agrees not to tell Triton on the grounds that Ariel would be denied her dream of living on the surface. Apparently washed up from a shipwreck, Ariel is taken in by Eric. Eric does not recognize her, but is often found playing the song he heard to the sea as a means of hailing the woman who saved him. Still, Eric and Ariel become fast friends. They spend the next day together exploring the kingdom, and the two almost kiss on a boat ride at the end of the day. They are thwarted by Ursula's eels, who tip the boat over. Dismayed at Ariel's progress, Ursula decides to complicate the situation by taking the form of a beautiful woman with Ariel's voice. Eric almost marries the disguised Ursula, much to Ariel's despair, but at the last minute her seagull friend Scuttle discovers Ursula's ruse and rallies the local animals to disrupt the wedding. In the confusion, Ursula drops and breaks her magical seashell, which contains Ariel's voice. Ariel regains her voice and Eric finally recognizes her as his rescuer. Unfortunately, he is unable to kiss her before the sun sets. Both Ariel and Ursula return to their true forms and to the sea.

At that moment, Triton arrives to confront Ursula and rescue Ariel. When faced with the binding contract between Ariel and Ursula, Triton signs a contract of his own. Under the terms of his deal with Ursula, he surrenders his freedom in exchange for Ariel's. He is transformed into a wretched slug like creature, and Ursula claims his crown, trident, and power over the sea. Eric, who has plunged into the sea to rescue Ariel, then throws a harpoon at Ursula. Ariel and Eric proceed to battle Ursula, culminating in the sea witch growing to enormous size and Eric impaling her with the prow of a sunken ship dredged up by her whirlpool. Eric is tossed into the sea, and Ariel once again carries him back to shore. A restored Triton, recognizing Ariel's love for Eric, transforms her back into a human. Eric and Ariel have a wedding attended by humans and merpeople alike, and begin a life together on the surface.

It's fair to say that *The Little Mermaid* largely created the Disney film as it is understood today. It takes the conventions of the classical Princess film and magnifies them to modern cinematic proportions. Take the film's remarkable music, for example. Music has always been an important part of Disney films. Even children who haven't seen *Snow White and The Seven Dwarfs* know all eight words of "Heigh Ho" through advertising or other forms of popular osmosis. Still, most classical Disney songs are very similar to "Heigh Ho." For the most part, the songs of this early period are highly sedate pieces. They're either simple catchy strands of tune meant to delight and amuse, or else choral arrangements, both in the sense of their vocal style and in the dramatic sense borrowed from Greek theater, that of an all-knowing voice describing the scene and setting the mood. Occasionally, the lines are blurred. Examples include Jiminy Cricket's solo interlude in "When You Wish Upon a Star" and Aurora's operatic vocals prior to meeting Phillip.

The Little Mermaid brings a whole new kind of music to Disney films, one fairly obviously influenced by composer Alan Menken's background in musical theater. Ariel and Ursula both deliver powerful and dynamic vocal performances in songs that inform the plot and invite the audience to immerse themselves in the characters' world. Beyond the songs themselves, the musical score achieves a richness never before equaled in a Disney film. The music is infused with the world itself, with the music of "Part of Your World" providing the first ever leitmotif of a Disney Princess film. It truly does set the new standard for all Disney music to come. Even the later films, which seem more akin to DreamWorks parodies than straightforward Disney films, follow the musical conventions laid out in this film. It's clear that the film is aware of its music's vital importance. Sebastian, in addition to being Ariel's reluctant companion, serves as Triton's court composer, and Ariel's singing voice is key in Eric recognizing her. The focus on music is somewhat ironic, given that for half of the film Ariel is unable to speak or sing. It is possible that such an irony is not only intentional, but essential for the flow of the story. Since there are large portions of time where the main character cannot talk, it becomes necessary for the music to provide a through line for the narrative.

Like the music, Ariel echoes Disney's past but brings a new spin to it. True to Disney Princess form, she is a young woman largely defined by her dreams and wishes. However, there are some important ways in which her dreams differ from those of Princesses before her. First of all, she has very specific dreams that don't involve marrying a prince. She does marry one, but he's really more of an extension of her dream of living on the surface than anything else. This is problematic in its own way, but it's important to establish at the outset that Ariel makes the mistakes she makes in pursuit of her own preferred lifestyle and not for the sake of a man. It's worth noting the significance of the fact that Ariel makes a mistake at all. It would be better if she learned something or underwent some kind of character development as the result of her mistakes, but her flawed character makes her a welcome departure from the purity of the earlier Princesses. As positive as Snow White and Cinderella might be, they are possessed of a certain demure and flawless righteousness that hinders the drama of their characters to a degree. Even if the resolution is lacking, the tension between Ariel and Triton does provide a relatable conflict in Ariel's personal life, and the fact of Ariel's deal with a monstrous sea witch gives her a greater sense of agency than Snow White and especially Aurora.

The other important thing about Ariel's dreams is that she actually pursues them. Even before she meets Eric, she spends most of her time scouring the ocean for treasures from the human world. What's more, she isn't content simply to collect items, she wants to understand how life in such a different world is possible. She asks fundamental questions such as why fire burns, as well as more specific ones like what a fork is used for, and she is constantly seeking knowledge. She makes frequent trips to the surface to speak to Scuttle about humans, and she even reads human books that somehow maintain their integrity underwater. She isn't presented as giving up any of her dreams for Eric's sake either. Even knowing that she has a limited time in which to make him fall in love with her, she doesn't let the urgency of her situation distract her from exploring the human world. While Ariel is a step in the right direction for women's roles in Disney films, she is far from unproblematic. The most nagging issue with Ariel is not that she allows her dreams to be defined by a man, but rather that she conflates her dreams with a man.

Ariel, like the Princesses before her, knows nothing about the man she has fallen in love with, but she thinks she does because she is projecting her feelings about humanity onto him.

According to the psychologist Jacques Lacan, such misdirected fascinations are a primary motivation for most or all romantic relationships and love for others is usually based on a sort of unwitting narcissism. There is a certain relevance to Lacan with respect to film, to be sure, but the fascinations he describes affect our personal relationships as well. Lacan believes that people project their feelings and identity onto others the same way they do onto the image of their own selves. They love other people not for who they are, but for that which they see of themselves in them. While Lacan's characterization of romantic love and the human psyche are highly debatable, his theories are a plausible enough explanation for the juvenile infatuation seen in this film. Ariel, like an infant beginning to be aware, has an image of herself which is unlike her own awkward body. She imagines the swimming allowed by her tail to be a poor trade for the dancing and jumping afforded to humans by their legs. She also projects herself into the human world and an imagined better life. She mentions at one point that she imagines humans not to have authoritarian parents like Triton, despite her admission that she actually knows very little about humans.

Ariel's curiosity about the human world is compelling, but one doesn't get the sense that she gives any serious thought to the things she discovers. She simply wonders at them for a moment and moves on to the next thing. This would perhaps be understandable if she didn't apply the same attitude to Eric. Not that Ariel is anything but steadfast in her affections, but her attitude toward Eric is one of wonder rather than appreciation. He's the first human male she's ever seen up close, and one gets the sense that he could just as easily have been any human. Indeed, Eric could be just about any human. His only discernable characteristics are his love for Ariel, a sense of humor, and a vaguely rebellious streak against the traditionalist current of nobility represented by Grimsby. The last is the only characteristic which Eric and Ariel might share, though the relationship between Grimsby and Eric is much less tense than the one between Ariel and Triton. This is probably due to the inverse of the power dynamic between the two. Grimsby is Eric's servant, not his father. Perhaps Ariel is attracted to Eric's power over Grimsby, as it plays into her fantasy of a less restricted life on the surface. There is a telling contrast between men and women in this comparison. Ariel, a woman, is under the authority of her male elder. Eric, a man, is possessed of an authority over his. This is one facet of the problematic image set by this film.

What little information about Eric's character is revealed is enough to show that Eric's statue is not a fitting representation of him. He is presented as a stalwart warrior, and while he does demonstrate some combat ability in the film's climax, it's fairly clear by his amusement with the statue and his actual physical stature that he is not the swaggering Hercules represented in stone. Yet, Ariel takes this image of Eric and projects her infatuation onto it, even saying that it looks just like him. She doesn't know Eric well enough to know that he is not accurately represented here, and it is thus made clear that she is in love with his image and the ideal that he represents and not the man himself. Her love for him is just another item in her collection. To the film's credit, certain plot points indicate that it is at least partially aware of this pattern of Lacanian fascination. Ariel's greatest obstacle to winning Eric's love is his own fascination with some surface element of Ariel's persona, her voice. He holds off on pursuing a relationship with her to find the woman with her voice, and he almost marries someone else because of this fascination. Ariel sees something of her own fantasies in an ideal version of Eric, and is almost thwarted by the ideal qualities he identifies her with. The problem with defending the film's narrative on these grounds is that Ariel is never given a chance to appreciate the irony of the situation. Ursula almost wins because Eric approaches love the same way Ariel does, but she never takes the next step and reevaluates her own approach in light of what she should be learning, but isn't. She doesn't necessarily have to not marry Eric, but perhaps the two could have some kind of character moment where they at least reassure each other that their marriage is a good idea.

Before applying the idea of the idealized self as a projection upon others in a more metafictional context to analyze the unfortunate gender roles promoted by Ariel, it is only fair to examine some of her more positive qualities. First of all, the relationship between her and Eric does actually take some time to develop. One can easily find fault with the speed of the development, with the pair ready to marry after only three days. Still, that's much longer than it takes any of the earlier Princesses to secure the love of their Prince. In addition, there are actually scenes where the couple is seen interacting and building a certain chemistry. Another positive thing about Ariel is her active nature compared with previous Princesses. As mentioned, her admittedly foolish deal with Ursula displays her agency, and she proves useful during the climactic battle. It might be Eric who ultimately kills

Ursula, but Ariel does an effective job of drawing her attention and even attacking her as a means of misdirecting her fire. She's the first Disney Princess who isn't utterly reliant on others to rescue her. Snow White needed the Dwarfs, Cinderella needed the mice, and Aurora needed Phillip. On top of all that, Ariel has the most well developed personality of any Disney Princess (for the time, anyway). She's passionate, she's curious, and she's rebellious. She actually puts one in mind of a teenager, if only a heavily stereotyped one.

Stereotypes are of course Ariel's downfall. Despite all of her positive qualities, she does play into many of the feminine conventions imposed upon the Princess archetype. Indeed, while Snow White might be the earliest example, Ariel is really responsible for the idea of the Disney Princess as she stands in the popular consciousness today. The truly insidious thing is that everything about Ariel's image and character seems to have been manipulated to make her the ideal marketing icon for Disney at the expense of her audience. First of all, it's important to understand the context in which Ariel was created, and why Disney returned to the Princess genre after 30 years. After *Sleeping Beauty*, Disney began a long series of films largely unconnected to fairy tales (though *The Black Cauldron* and to a lesser extent *The Sword in the Stone* fall under the category of classical fantasy). Most of these films had two things in common: a heavy focus on animal characters that would later cause Disney executives to erroneously predict a poor box office return on *The Lion King*[1] and a very

---

[1] See the featurette "Origins" included with the 2003 DVD release of *The Lion King*

rough and sketchy animation style. The pioneer example of this style is actually found in *Sleeping Beauty* in the form of Phillip's horse Samson. Whether or not either of these factors were truly responsible for the decline in sales that Disney experienced as the decades wore on, particularly in the 1980s when they were under intense competition from Don Bluth and his animation studio, *The Little Mermaid* tries very hard to avoid the conventions that had characterized Disney films for a long time.

There is a concentrated effort to create a new art style for Disney, namely the big eyes and smooth lines that are traditionally associated with the Disney art style today. Arguably, the change is only really successful in the "Part of Your World" number. At other times, particularly in scenes where Ariel is on the surface but near water, the faces of the characters always seem to vibrate and warp slightly with extra lines. The return to this sort of Princess story is a return to Disney's roots, and it is timed beautifully to coincide with the expansion of the home video market that saw the return of all the classic Princess films to a new audience. When comparing Ariel to the other Princesses, two very interesting differences can be discerned. Both of these traits serve largely to enhance the marketability of the Disney brand.

Ariel is the first Disney Princess to actually grow up amid royal luxury. All the previous Princesses live as servants in their own homes, live as peasants in the forest, or both. Ariel lives relatively contently in a palace. In addition to the potential for a dramatically satisfying familial relationship between important characters, this point also gives the potential for palace playsets and nautically themed accessories. Such a thing is not at all out of place in the 1980s, when several animated television shows were created for the express purpose of selling toys. Such a materialistic subtext is only exacerbated by Ariel's fixation on collecting treasure.

Taking to heart the adage that sex sells, *The Little Mermaid* is also one of the most sexualized Disney films in existence. Some instances are a little difficult to spot, like Ariel's arched back and thrusting torso at the end of her "Part of Your World" reprise. Others are much more overt, such as an extreme close up of Ursula's jiggling breasts. Of course the sexualization of cinematic characters is not necessarily a detriment, but in this film it becomes problematic because the sexual undertones are not present for the sake of entertaining the audience. They are incorporated into the film as part of the image being sold to the children who watch it. Little girls are invited to compare themselves to a highly sexual mermaid who luxuriates amid opulence and treasure and find themselves lacking.

Despite the damning criticism of the last few pages and the mixed reputation that the film has garnered for Disney, it is important to note that *The Little Mermaid* is motivated by a genuine spark of artistry at least as much as it is by corporate greed and the need to sell the Princess image. Despite the dubious nature of the story that holds them together, the music and animation of this film are truly spectacular. It's highly unlikely that when Alan Menken wrote this film's moving and haunting score, his only thought was how to brainwash young girls. Besides, to ascribe to this film the power to genuinely warp the minds of youth denies the ability of children to form their own judgments and values. Still, *The Little Mermaid* has become a symbol that encapsulates many common complaints against Disney, and it is fortunate that the studio followed this film with two of the most robust and compelling Princesses in their canon.

Beauty and the Beast

Beauty and The Beast is one of Disney's most acclaimed films, being the first animated film to be nominated for the Academy Award for Best Picture. It is also the last straightforward fairy tale to be produced by Disney, with all films following including parodic elements or being outside the genre altogether. This doesn't mean that films to follow have no adherence to or bearing upon the conventions of the Disney romantic film, merely that this is the last film to deal seriously with the themes of princesses, dreams, and love as a magical force.

Ten years before the story begins, a spoiled prince turns away an old woman seeking shelter in his castle. Revealing herself to be an enchantress, the woman transforms the Prince into a monstrous Beast and all his servants into animate furniture and appliances. She leaves him with a rose that will begin to wilt on his 20th birthday. If he can find mutual romantic love before the rose wilts completely, he and his servants will return to normal.

The story begins with a bookish young woman named Belle resisting the romantic advances of Gaston, her village's resident hunter and most respected man. An explosion at her house draws her away from the conversation to the house she shares with her father Maurice, a local inventor with a well-deserved reputation for eccentricity. Maurice has encountered some difficulty with his automated wood chopper, but is able to fix it with some encouragement from Belle. While taking his machine to a fair in another village, Maurice loses his horse Philippe and is chased by wolves to the Beast's castle. He receives hospitable treatment from the servants, but the Beast responds to the disturbance with anger and imprisons him. After Belle flat out refuses to marry Gaston, Philippe comes back without Maurice and Belle follows him to the castle. Once there, she exchanges her freedom for her father's.

In hopes of winning Belle's affections and breaking the spell, the Beast gives her a comfortable room and free range of the castle with the exception of the west wing, where he hides the enchanted rose. Initially put off by the Beast's temperamental and demanding attitude, Belle is at least able to make friends with the servants. After inducing them to take her on a tour of the castle, she comes across the west wing. Eluding the servants, she opens an imposing door to find a darkened room full of smashed furniture. In the midst of the wreckage, she sees the rose and almost touches it. The Beast stops her before she can, and rages at her. Frightened, she flees the castle and is attacked by a pack of wolves. The Beast arrives to save her, but is injured in the process. Grateful and ever compassionate, Belle takes him back to the castle and nurses him back to health. Meanwhile, Maurice arrives in the village and tries to organize a rescue for Belle. He is laughed out of the town tavern, and Gaston hits upon the idea of blackmailing Belle into marriage by threatening to lock her father up in an asylum. Determined to rescue Belle on his own, Maurice sets off for the castle again.

Over a vaguely defined period of time, Belle and the Beast become close friends as her kindness brings out his gentler nature. One night, after the two share a romantic dance, Belle expresses a desire to see her father again. The Beast reveals a magic hand

mirror given to him by the enchantress that will allow the holder
to see whatever they wish. Seeing her father sick and dying in the
forest, Belle is distraught. Out of love for her, the Beast lets her
leave the castle. He gives her the mirror in hopes she will use it to
remember the time they've had together. Chip, the child turned
tea cup, stows away in Belle's bag hoping to convince her to return.

Belle brings her father home, and Gaston arrives to enact
his blackmail. Belle uses the mirror to prove her father's sanity
by showing the townspeople the Beast. Led by Gaston, they form
a mob to attack the castle and slay the Beast. Belle and Maurice
are locked in their home, but manage to escape with the help of
Chip and Maurice's machine. The servants beat back the mob, but
Gaston takes advantage of the confusion to slip away and find the
Beast. Despondent, the Beast allows Gaston to shoot him and kick
him to the edge of a precipice. Upon seeing Belle ride up to the
castle, the Beast fights back, but chooses at the last moment to not
throw Gaston off the castle. The Beast climbs up to a balcony where
Belle is waiting and is stabbed in the back by Gaston, who loses his
balance and falls to his doom. Belle confesses her love to the dying
Beast just before the rose's last petal falls. Magical lights fall from
the sky, returning the Beast and his servants to their human forms.
Belle and the Beast then live happily ever after in the castle.

Right from the beginning the film establishes itself as an
enhanced version of classical Disney fairy tales with the use of
visual parallels. The prologue in stained glass is reminiscent of the
establishing narration for *Sleeping Beauty*, which is accompanied
by pictures from a physical storybook. Such a method of
introducing stories was common in Disney films of the time,

even those that didn't feature fairytale subject matter. *The Jungle Book* is one example of the convention's use in a different genre. Still, this method is used to greatest effect in *Sleeping Beauty*. The medieval tapestry style of the illustrations in the book serves as a fine preview of the film's art style, and the combination of those illustrations and the visible text that mirrors the spoken words of the narrator create a clear disconnect between reality and fantasy that prepares the viewer for the broad strokes of the dreamlike experience to come.

Beauty and the Beast takes this same formula and plays with it to establish a world which is more concerned than *Sleeping Beauty* with its internal logic and the personal struggles of its characters. The establishing shot of the entire film is not a bejeweled book on a reading stand, but rather a bucolic forest with a gurgling waterfall. This simple change signals to the audience that while this film adheres to the trappings and environs of a classical fairy tale, it is to be understood as a world unto itself rather than a storybook. This might seem like an incredibly minor cue, but it drastically changes the way the audience relates to the story. Suddenly, the audience that came expecting a flight of fancy is prepared for the characters to act like real people with their own lives and interests.

This focus on characters and the immersion in their world is reinforced as the prologue moves into the stained glass sequence. The images of the events which set up the story are presented not as illustrations of a book, but as windows in the Beast's castle. While it is unlikely that these particular windows are actually present in the castle, unless perhaps the entire story is told in flashback from a time after the enchantment was lifted, the point is made clear that the events about to be seen are a part of whatever world we have entered. The narrator's delivery contributes to the atmosphere of authenticity as well. Unlike the *Sleeping Beauty* narrator, he doesn't sound like he's setting up a conflict. He has the tone of a man describing an actual tragic circumstance. His voice is labored with emotion and his older voice gives the reading a rough quality, like that of a wise old man recounting an anecdote.

Beyond the content of the visuals and the performance, the frame itself enhances the emotional immersion of the film. The stained glass images are not presented flatly. We do not simply see one window before moving on to the next. Instead, the interlude makes wonderful use of classical editing, described in Giannetti's *Understanding Movies*[1] as the juxtaposition of medium, long, and close shots in order to accentuate the action and emotional content of a scene. The sequence starts with a long shot establishing the Prince and his castle, but as the scene goes on it includes close ups of the old woman, the rose, and the Beast's hands as he transforms. There are also some slow and stylized zooms in the scene which add to its dynamism. Of course, earlier Disney films also made ample use of these editing and framing techniques. Such juxtapositions are arguably the foundation on which all mainstream cinema has been based since the early 1900s. However, the use of these techniques here, upon stained glass in a prologue to a fairy tale, is a truly novel thing for Disney.

The increased emphasis on immersion and character in *Beauty and the Beast* may be attributable to the influence of the

---

[1] *Understanding Movies*, 13th ed. New York: Pearson, 2014. See Chapter 4, "Editing," on page 135.

Broadway musical, an art form famous for melodrama and the use of sweeping music to express the inner thoughts and feelings of characters. This influence is felt most heavily in the opening song, which goes beyond the heavy use of formal musical theater devices such as spoken interludes over the musical bridges and the large cast that breaks down at one point into singing unconnected phrases that are arranged to gel harmoniously. The song deals with the firm establishment of Belle's life and the concerns of her village home—territory that has not been explored by any prior Disney song. The opening song introduces the protagonist and the main villain and also the community they live in. We get to see Belle interact with the people in her native environment, which is something that hasn't been done with any Disney Princess before. Seeing Belle go about some sort of daily business not only makes her a well-rounded character, it also properly contextualizes her fascination with fantasy and mystery.

Like Cinderella, Belle's specific dreams are never known, but that has to do with Belle not being able to fully grasp them herself. An important part of Belle's character arc is deciding for herself exactly how her vague desires for something greater will manifest themselves. In a refreshing change from Snow White and Aurora, her aspirations pointedly do not involve male validation. The only time she even broaches the subject is in the opening song, when telling some sheep about the book she's immersed in. She describes the main character meeting Prince Charming as her favorite part of the story. Still, her enthusiasm has less to do with the Prince himself and more to do with the mystery surrounding his identity and the heroine's future discovery of just who he is. Besides her seemingly infinite compassion, Belle's other main characteristic is her curiosity. In the Beast's castle, she can't resist the allure of what might be hidden in the forbidden west wing. The story Belle reads is clearly meant to parallel the main narrative of the film. This parallel is communicated musically as Belle and the Beast get better acquainted. The song which montages their growing friendship features a reprise of the musical cue in which Belle remarks upon her book. It's a fair assumption that Belle models herself after the characters in her books to a degree. She does, after all, project herself into her books when contemplating her desire to experience something beyond her mundane life in the village.

The most salient thing about Belle's relationship to her stories and dreams is that she recognizes them as such. She may take some inspiration from her magical fictional worlds, but she remains practical with respect to her own life. What's more, she doesn't allow herself to fall into the destructive norms of her culture. The whole town gossips about her odd bookish behavior, but she pays them no mind and firmly resolves to be her own person, and when Gaston attempts to propose marriage, she is able to effectively deter him. From the outset, Belle appears to be a very positive role model. She's active, intelligent, and self-reliant, all while maintaining compassion and a sense of wonder.

Shifting focus onto the film's villain, Gaston is also a very interesting character. Unlike many Disney villains, he isn't motivated by power or revenge or jealousy. Gaston is already the most respected man in his village, and deservedly so. As a skilled hunter, he provides the village with a valuable service. What's more, he is in a position where he is more or less content. He can hunt as much as he wants, and he could have his pick of almost any young woman in the village. If he could just respect Belle's autonomy, he could probably live a happy and productive life. Gaston's fatal flaw is his sense of entitlement. He feels that because of his status within the community and physical prowess he is deserving of Belle's affections. To a certain extent, he falls prey to the same Lacanian fascination that clouds the judgment of Ariel. He sees himself as the most beautiful man in town, and Belle as the most beautiful woman (though he patronizingly refers to her as a girl). Gaston sees Belle's great beauty as a feminine reflection of himself, and it is for that reason he desires her, rather than because of any qualities intrinsic to Belle herself. Note that when he first announces his intention to marry Belle, he almost loses her in the crowd at the marketplace because she passes him while he is distracted by the beauty of his own reflection.

It's fairly clear that Gaston requires the validation of a female counterpart in order to feel secure with himself. He directly equates Belle's beauty with her worth, and he seems to see beauty as the primary source of his own worth as well. The first time he bullies his lackey Le Fou on screen, it is in the context of asking Le Fou to verify that he deserves the village's most beautiful woman, and when Belle rejects his marriage proposal he refers to himself as a disgrace. To a certain extent, perhaps Gaston recognizes his own shallowness, and his despair comes from the knowledge that if Belle is not induced to marry him by his looks alone he has nothing else to offer her. Of course, Gaston does have positive traits as well. He does possess a great deal of skill and self-discipline in his own way. Sadly, he lacks the self-awareness to realize that he is unappealing to Belle not because of any failing of his own, but rather because he views Belle as a metric of his success rather than her own person. Gaston describes his vision of a perfect married life to Belle, which consists largely of her service to him and his male children. He gives no thought to the idea that Belle might have her own life plans, and he certainly has no notion of being any kind of life partner to her. He doesn't even consult with her before arranging their wedding.

The episode of Gaston's attempted surprise marriage to Belle serves as one example of Gaston as a metaphor for the traditional Prince Charming. There are many ways in which Gaston mirrors Prince Phillip, the most recognizable Prince from the pre-renaissance Disney era. The most questionable scene to feature Phillip is the conversation between him and Aurora leading up to their dance in the forest. After watching her dance with the animals who have absconded with his cape and boots, Phillip begins dancing with her without communicating with her first. Understandably startled to find herself dancing with a stranger, Aurora tries to distance herself from him. Philip proceeds to grab hold of her hand and stop her. Naturally, Philip's behavior is highly inappropriate in any kind of real world situation, but the questionable nature of his style of flirtation is masked behind fairytale trappings of dreams and destiny.

Beauty and the Beast, being a film much more committed to the honest exploration of believable characters, dispenses with the dazzling magical mystique when Gaston enters Belle's home. Sensing her initial reluctance, Gaston adopts predatory tactics. He aggressively swaggers toward Belle and makes every attempt to corner her.

Gaston is also similar to Philip in that his primary vocation is violence. Unlike Philip, his violence is not valorous. His fear mongering crusade against the Beast is driven by the need to display is own prowess, not a genuine desire to protect his fellow villagers. Even his hunting, which serves the useful purpose of providing the community with food and furs, doesn't involve the sort of heroism that Phillip exemplifies. Again, Gaston's character is the result of dressing down the archetype of the Disney Prince as befits a more realistic context. Even Gaston's design is a subtle nod to Disney's past. Most of the other characters in the film are drawn with smooth lines and simple shapes. Gaston's bulging muscles and chiseled features give him more lines in his design than the other characters, and a sketchy quality reminiscent of older Disney films from the 1960s to the 1980s. It is important to realize, however, that while Gaston offers a skewed perspective on conventional fairytale masculinity, he is not a parodic character. Despite his witlessness and chauvinism being played for laughs occasionally, Gaston and the danger he represents to Belle and the Beast are taken very seriously for most of the film.

Naturally, Gaston's sense of entitlement makes him the perfect antagonist for the Beast because their personality flaws mirror one another. Gaston objectifies Belle by reducing her to a romantic trophy, and the Beast's servants are literally objects. Interestingly, the objects that the servants become seem to mirror the functions they served for the Prince when they were human. The chef becomes an oven, the maid becomes a duster, and Lumiere, who appears to be the Beast's butler, may well have carried candelabras for the Prince. In other words, the servants become the simple appliances that the spoiled Prince always viewed them as. If one hypothesizes that the enchantment over the castle was modeled after the Prince's perceptions of the people around him, it follows that even before the transformation the Prince had a monstrous self-image. In any case, the Beast has certainly internalized his monstrosity by the time the film proper begins. His first assumption at Maurice's intrusion is that the intruder has come to the castle to gawk at him. While waiting for Belle to attend their first dinner together, he discusses the hopelessness of his situation with his servants, citing Belle's beauty and comparing it to his hideous visage.

The Beast's self-image also plays a part, appropriately enough, in the function of his magic mirror. The mirror allows the user to see whatever they wish, and yet it usually shows the user exactly what they expect to see. When Gaston uses the mirror to view the Beast, he sees a roaring and fearsome monster. His perception of the Beast could be said to be influenced by his role as a hunter, seeing the Beast as an animal to be conquered. Since prowess and swagger are the primary methods by which he interacts with the world, he perceives the Beast as roaring to display dominance and ferocity rather than despair and loneliness. Conversely, when the Beast uses the mirror to observe Belle, he sees her expressing her hatred of him to the wardrobe in her room. The Beast, convinced already of the hopelessness of the situation, takes this as a sign that Belle will never love him. Were he not so mired in melancholy, he might take Belle's attitude as the result of her abduction and his abrasiveness rather than his mere existence. The Beast's low self-image serves to generate sympathy in the audience, and while it doesn't excuse his cruelty to Belle and his servants, it does make his redemption more palatable. Note that this sympathy is not mirrored in Gaston's lament of his desire to woo Belle. This is because Gaston's insecurity stems from a challenge to his supposed superiority, not a seeming confirmation of his inferiority.

Gaston and the Beast share a sense of entitlement, but there are two key differences between the two characters. The first is that the Beast's enchantment has served as a revelation of sorts. He's had many years to reflect upon his failings, and appears to have an interest in bettering himself beyond just returning to human form. When waiting for Belle to come to dinner, he doesn't just complain that Belle isn't doing what he wants. He expresses frustration with his own inability to persuade her to accept his attentions. The Beast's focus on self-improvement gives him an arc that the audience can get heavily invested in, given that they have borne witness to both his cruelty and his contriteness already. Gaston should have received a similar epiphany and taken stock of his life when Belle rejected his marriage proposal, but he only concocts a scheme to force Belle to marry him rather than committing to making himself into a person that she could love. This marks him as the villain and the Beast as the hero, or at least the one the audience wants to see become a hero.

The other key difference is in the very nature of their entitlement. Gaston has the air of a man who has always gotten what he wants through his strength and good looks and always expects to receive it. As demonstrated by the scene in Belle's home, Gaston's manner is practiced and predatory. The Beast, by contrast, has an entitlement more akin to a spoiled child. One outstanding example is the Beast's attitude when denying Belle's pleas for Maurice's freedom. The Beast petulantly refuses to free Maurice on the grounds that the man is his prisoner, as though Maurice were a toy or a piece in a game. The Beast has a distinct lack of empathy, but he is utterly without guile. The similarity to a child's behavior makes sense, as the Beast got everything he wanted just for being born who he is, and not because of any cultivated attitudes. Not to mention, he received his epiphany at a much younger age.

Even though the Beast's journey is one of maturity, and Belle is his role model for learning the compassion and empathy of a well-rounded adult, Belle should not be confused with a mother figure. The enchanted teakettle Mrs. Potts much better fills that role in the Beast's life. She provides unfailing counsel and support to the Beast, yet remains firm when confronting him with his flaws. Perhaps most importantly, Belle doesn't ultimately have any responsibility to help the Beast better himself. His fortunes, and those of his servants, are riding on his being able to overcome his own faults. Not even Mrs. Potts or the other servants can make him learn to love or make Belle love him. Intriguingly, the Beast learns to respect Belle's autonomy before the servants do. They see Belle primarily as a means of lifting their curse, and are flabbergasted when the Beast releases her despite the fact that her imprisonment is reprehensible in the first place. The servants have this attitude toward Belle right from the beginning. They even refer to her as a girl the same way Gaston does. With the exception of Mrs. Potts, who reminds Lumiere that such things as romance cannot be rushed, they expect her to fall in love with the Beast as a matter of course and very quickly.

There is a certain ambiguity about just how long the courtship does take. It lasts at least a few days, but it could take months. The snow begins to fall when Belle arrives at the castle, and is thawing when the mob attacks, but at the same time it's hard to believe Maurice was unable to find the castle again for an entire season. Still, Maurice doesn't have the best sense of direction, and the thaw could be explained away by a heat wave. This temporal ambiguity is also present in the magical rose. It is established that ten years pass between the enchantment being cast and broken. It is also established that the rose blooms until the Beast's 20th birthday. It is not established how long it takes the rose to wilt, thus leaving the age of the Beast open to interpretation. He could be anywhere from 20 to 30, though it seems more likely that he is on the younger side of his third decade given his childlike demeanor. In both cases, the temporal ambiguity serves to take focus off of fairytale constructs and onto the characters. The filmmakers cleverly avoid the criticism that comes with Ariel getting married at the age of 16, or to a man she only met a few days ago. By making such details as the characters' ages and their length of time together vague, the film makes it clear that what matters is the development and character of their relationship.

Belle and the Beast, even though their relationship comes to fruition over just one montage of screen time, are one of the most effective Disney couples because they have something to offer each other. Belle teaches the Beast to let go of his sense of entitlement, and he offers her the understanding companion she expresses a desire for early in the film. At first glance, it might seem that Belle is giving far more than she's receiving. However, such an understanding person is a real rarity in her life. Between the gossipy townsfolk, the boorish Gaston, and her lovable but clueless father who actually thinks marriage to Gaston is a good idea, the Beast is probably the first person Belle has ever met who is sensitive to her needs (with the possible exception of the old man in the bookshop).

The ultimate question at the heart of *Beauty and the Beast*'s story and characters is whether the deeper romance and better rounded personalities in an unapologetically fantastic universe marks the film as the beginning of the Disney romance's revisionist phase, or the apex of the classical phase. Leaving aside that such distinctions are ultimately arbitrary, the answer depends largely on what exactly it means to be a classical Disney romance. If what is most essential to the genre is the extrapolation of the flighty romance of fairy tales into a rich cinematic experience with enchanting music, endearing characters, and riveting plots revolving around intense moments of love and fear, then *Beauty and the Beast* is the classical Disney romance at its most sophisticated. If the genre derives its identity from the perpetuation of fairytale stereotypes, the vicarious thrill of the whirlwind love affair, and the seductive escape into a simpler opiated world of dreams, then *Beauty and the Beast* represents the first significant break with these conventions.

Either way, the film marks a turning point for Disney. For a long while after, Disney would take its product much more seriously. Their characters would be much more fleshed out, they would experiment with bold new territory for storytelling, and they would examine their signature romance formula from many interesting angles.

Aladdin

Aladdin is a very interesting offering from the Disney Renaissance for several reasons. For one thing, it is the only animated Disney film of this era to feature a male protagonist. It is also the only film to feature a Disney Princess who is not the main character. (With the possible exception of *Sleeping Beauty*, which plays out more as a conflict between the good and evil fairies than between any of the human characters.) The film also heralds a major shift in the humorous aspects of animated films in general. The pop culture references and modern speech patterns employed by Robin Williams as the voice of the Genie are a clear precursor to the humor of animated films today.

Aladdin features as its main character a boy living on the streets of the fantasy city of Agrabah. After outwitting the guards, sharing the bread he stole with urchin children, and being publicly berated by the latest suitor for Princess Jasmine, Aladdin reflects on his desire to transcend his poverty and prove himself a worthy person. Unknown to Aladdin, the magical Cave of Wonders already considers him worthy. In fact, he is the only one worthy to enter the cave and retrieve a magical lamp. Jafar, a sorcerer in the employ of Agrabah's Sultan, wants to use the lamp's power to usurp the throne.

Meanwhile, Princess Jasmine resists her father's forcing her to marry a prince. She runs away from the palace in disguise, but her inexperience with the outside world leads her into a dangerous situation when she inadvertently steals from an apple cart. Fortunately, Aladdin is nearby and rescues her by convincing the vendor that she is insane. By this time, Jafar has determined Aladdin's identity and arranges to have him locked up so he can take him to the Cave of Wonders. Just as Aladdin and Jasmine are getting acquainted, they become involved in a chase whereby Aladdin is captured and Jasmine's identity is revealed. Aladdin is infatuated with Jasmine, but believes that marriage to her is off limits because of his social station. Jafar, disguised as an old man, tells him about the fabulous treasure in the Cave of Wonders and offers to help him escape if he retrieves the lamp.

Aladdin finds the lamp, and a sentient flying carpet, but becomes trapped during a cave-in. Denied the lamp, Jafar decides to become Sultan by marrying Jasmine himself. Having survived the cave-in, Aladdin discovers that the lamp contains a genie who can grant him three wishes. He uses the Genie's magic to make himself a prince. He is successful in convincing Jasmine to marry him, and even exposes Jafar as a traitor. Unfortunately, Jafar discovers that Aladdin has the lamp. After Aladdin hesitates in freeing the Genie as he had earlier promised, Jafar seizes the opportunity and steals the lamp from him. Jafar uses the Genie to become Sultan and vastly increase his magical power, but is defeated when Aladdin tricks him into wishing to be a genie himself. Jafar becomes trapped in his own lamp, and is sealed in the Cave of Wonders. Jasmine and Aladdin are allowed to marry, and the Genie is set free.

Perhaps the most interesting aspect of Aladdin, and the aspect most relevant to our discussion of romance in Disney films, is the theming of the story, both explicit and subtextual. The stated theme of the movie is personal authenticity. The Genie frequently advises Aladdin to be himself, Aladdin's identity gives him an inherent worth that transcends his societal label of street rat, and he is ultimately able to defeat Jafar by trickery. In this way, Aladdin calls back to the skills he used to acquire food and clemency from merchants in the first act of the film. Not only is this a clever bit of storytelling, it also serves as an affirmation of Aladdin's identity. When denied the help of the Genie in the climactic scene, Aladdin reclaims the label of street rat.

This theming of authenticity is all well and good, and "Be yourself" is certainly an easy catchphrase for young viewers to take to heart, but in certain ways it doesn't really make sense as an overarching theme for the film. After all, Aladdin doesn't start out pretending to be someone he isn't. He doesn't adopt the guise of Prince Ali Ababwa until half-way through the film. Before that, his primary obstacle to marrying Jasmine isn't his inauthenticity. She seems quite taken with his kind and clever personality almost from the moment they meet. Rather, the issue is that he isn't a prince. At first, this might seem like sloppy writing. Having overcome the primary obstacle of his social status, the writers invent a new obstacle by having Aladdin put on princely airs in order to elongate the story. But if the writing is that sloppy, why does the story still feel dramatically satisfying? Well, think about the most affirmative and beautiful scenes in this film. Which scene has the most sweeping score, the highest key lighting, and the greatest sense of triumph and resolution? It isn't the magic carpet ride, or the defeat of Jafar. It's the scene where the Genie is granted his freedom. This is the scene where all of the main characters have their respective arcs fulfilled. This scene is a highly appropriate and satisfying resolution because the theme of authenticity is just a small part of a larger and more subtle theme about the nature of freedom and its relationship to a societal power structure. The overemphasis on being oneself could be the result of a troublesome idea about children's film and television, the idea that a children's movie needs to say outright what it's about, that teaching lessons is more important than teaching the complex and powerful truths of moral maturity. The importance of authenticity is a much easier concept to convey to children than the complicated and highly debatable nature of freedom, even if the specifics of the simple theme are much less applicable to real life than those of the complex one.

This theme of freedom not only makes *Aladdin* one of Disney's best cinematic romances, it also makes for one of the most intricate interpersonal dynamics in all of animation. The three principle characters of the film are Aladdin, Jasmine, and the Genie. All of them want freedom, but they each want a different kind of freedom. Aladdin wants freedom of opportunity. He feels that he is worth something despite what society tells him and he wants a chance to prove it. Of course, his nominal motivation is to marry Jasmine, but even after this goal is within reach he remains unsatisfied. Because he never had the opportunity to prove his worth without the aid of magical deception, he feels that his position is not secure. If the truth were ever discovered, he fears, he would lose everything he has gained. It is only after he defeats Jafar despite his exposure as a fraud that he feels fulfilled. He overcomes the problem without any magical help, and even uses his intellect to defeat the very power which he had previously used to attain his opportunity. The Sultan doesn't just allow Aladdin to marry Jasmine out of gratitude, but because Aladdin has demonstrated that hereditary social standing is totally arbitrary and that many people can prove themselves if given a chance.

If Aladdin wants freedom of opportunity, Jasmine desires freedom from arbitrary and unfair societal restrictions. Despite her immense privilege, she is denied any autonomy because of her gender. The one concession made to her free will is that she is allowed to select which prince she marries. It's worth noting that the Sultan, who forces Jasmine into this situation, is never portrayed as malicious toward his daughter. When presented with the alternative of selecting a husband for Jasmine, he balks. He wishes only the best for his daughter, but is not wise enough to question the status quo until the end of the film. He wants a husband to take care of her, and it simply never enters his mind that she might be able to care for herself.

One of the most subtle bits of character development comes in the scene where the exposition of Jasmine's predicament occurs. Jasmine is holding and admiring a dove which lives in an elaborate bird cage in the palace garden. As the Sultan explains his desire for her to have a caring and providing husband, he absentmindedly takes the dove from her and places it back in the secure bird cage. There's no dialog referencing this action, but it's clear from Jasmine's expression as she walks off screen that she is frustrated. The Sultan has a highly protective nature, which is admirable in a parent, but his misguided effort threatens to take away any satisfaction his daughter might wring out of life. Tellingly, Jasmine immediately proceeds to play with some fish in the fountain, which is an open container beyond the Sultan's ability to close. This is a wonderful moment of animated acting. Jasmine's desire for the companionship of the fish motivates her presence at the fountain, which allows the striking visual of her splashing and turning her back on her royal reflection.

Despite not being the main character, Jasmine remains highly proactive in the film's narrative. The early scenes of the film might focus on Aladdin's daily life and desire for something greater, but the plot is set in motion by Jasmine's defiant escape from the palace. Jasmine isn't just sought out by Aladdin. She meets him as a result of her own actions. She has her own motivations and desires, and is not simply the fulfillment of Aladdin's character arc. She makes this point abundantly clear to Aladdin shortly after he arrives at the palace in disguise. Aladdin's efforts to court Jasmine fail utterly until he acknowledges this fact, and when Aladdin affirms her desire for autonomy the audience knows that his affirmation is sincere because autonomy was the one advantage Aladdin enjoyed in his life on the streets of Agrabah.

This key point explains why the romance between Jasmine and Aladdin works. Each one has and appreciates the form of freedom that the other yearns for, and they are both very kind individuals who reach out to another person to find what they lack. This also makes Jafar a perfect villain to oppose these characters. Jafar wants many of the same things as the lead couple. His desire to achieve a station in society greater than his own directly mirror's Aladdin's, and he and Jasmine both chafe under the rule of the buffoonish Sultan. The key difference with Jafar is that he is entirely self-contained. He doesn't seek personal connections with others and sees them entirely as a means to an end. Arguably, the primary cause of Jafar's downfall is his consistent underestimation of Aladdin. He needs Aladdin to retrieve the lamp, but is unprepared for Aladdin's trickery because he dismisses the boy as someone to be used and discarded, ignoring the Cave's seeming warning that Aladdin has intrinsic merit. Note also that like Aladdin and Jasmine, Jafar uses disguise to further his plans. Unlike them, he doesn't use a disguise to make contact with the larger world or another person. He does it for the sake of manipulation.

He also exploits Aladdin's affection for Jasmine, seeing love as just another tool to use against his foes. This is similar to the way the villainous Iago plays upon the title character's affection for Desdemona in Shakespeare's *Othello*—note that Jafar's parrot minion is named after this villain of classic theater. Like Iago, Jafar seems to consider himself above feelings of attraction. Once his plan to get the Genie's lamp fails, he pursues marriage to Jasmine purely as a means of political advancement. He plans to murder both Jasmine and her father once he has secured the throne. Later in the film, he proposes marriage to Jasmine after he has already become Sultan. His plan has changed because he now has mighty sorcerous magic to wield as power over Jasmine. He is more likely motivated by a desire to exercise this power than any sort of physical attraction. The only interpersonal relationship that Jafar seems to understand is one person's domination over another. If one observes his treatment of the Genie, their interactions feature a great deal of physical aggression on Jafar's part. He throws the Genie to the ground to tread upon his face, yanks harshly on his beard, and even coils around him while in snake form. Two important points about these instances are apparent: they all feature intense close-ups of Jafar in order to dramatically emphasize his aggression, and they all happen in response to Genie's verbal resistance to Jafar.

All of this makes the third act of the film appropriately jarring due to the stark contrast with Aladdin's treatment of the Genie as a friend and, more basically, as a person. The Genie exposits his desire for freedom after Aladdin asks him what he would wish for, something that apparently no one has ever asked him before. This says something about not only Aladdin but the world around him. It communicates to the audience that someone who sees people as complex beings with their own aspirations and perspectives is something of a rarity in the world of the film. This is hardly difficult to believe, given what we see of Jafar, the child-whipping Prince Achmed, and the palace guards who are wholly unsympathetic to Aladdin's plight. When Aladdin falters in fulfilling his promise to free the Genie, he comes perilously close to falling into this poisonous mode of thinking himself. The only thing that saves Aladdin is his conscience. We see not only from Aladdin's earlier interactions with the Genie but also from how troubled he is by the notion of someone being forced to marry that the curtailing of free will is a fundamental compromise of his core values. The idea that someone else must lose all hope of a better life so that he can continue to enjoy personal success tears him up inside. Aladdin is only able to secure an honest future together with Jasmine when he frees the Genie and affirms the values which he shares with Jasmine.

The movie's commentary on the nature of freedom is of course highly relevant to the real world, and serves as a fine counter-example for anyone who doubts Disney's social awareness. The film skillfully parses out different notions of freedom. It demonstrates through Aladdin and Jasmine that freedom of choice and freedom from restriction are fundamentally different but it also uses the Genie to remind the audience that these are descended from a more basic freedom, an essential personhood and dignity that most take for granted. The film doesn't chide Aladdin and Jasmine for their desires. It inspires and rewards them, and the audience, with the most awesome and magical example of their desires made manifest. The film calls upon the audience to observe the glory of freedom, and then reach out to those around us and spread this glory across the world.

Through their adventures, Aladdin and Jasmine become more than lovers. They are true partners. There are three key scenes where their romantic development is furthered. The first is their conversation in Aladdin's home, the second is the fabulous magic carpet ride, and the third is the freeing of the Genie and the Sultan's blessing of their marriage. Note that each of these scenes take place at the end of one of the film's acts and that each takes place approximately one day after the last. Though sequels to the film reveal that no marriage occurs for a long time, the fact of the couple's marriage is heavily implied in the original film. Three days is an unacceptably short engagement period for anyone living in the real world, but in most other ways Aladdin and Jasmine portray a very positive and healthy vision of romantic love.

Consider the first of these scenes. After the pair work together to escape a dangerous situation, they share a peaceful moment at Aladdin's house. At this point, Aladdin is already infatuated with Jasmine. How she feels in return is not as clear, but at the very least her body language makes her appear to be aware of and receptive to his infatuation. A basic physical attraction between the two makes sense. They are both good looking individuals with a good deal of intelligence and capability. The romantic mood of the scene is accompanied by the soft purple-pink lighting and the melodic score. This is the first time in the film that a soft, blended color has been used in the lighting. Prior to this, the lights have been a succession of high-key flat lighting schemes or hard and pervasive blue or red lights. The music is also in contrast with an earlier scene. It has the same melody as the musical number "One Jump," but with more of a soft lullaby quality than bounce or energy.

As the couple make their way to Aladdin's home, the close-ups become more and more common, giving the audience a sense of intimacy. The scene has clear romantic aesthetic cues, but what about the words and actions of the characters? Before they are interrupted by the guards, Aladdin and Jasmine are preparing to kiss. This intimacy is preceded by a discussion about the pros and cons of palace life. The conversation is hypothetical of course, since Jasmine's identity remains a secret until the conclusion of the guards' pursuit. Through an exploration of this issue, they come to realize that they both have some idea of what it is to feel trapped by their lot in life. This is the moment where a real connection is made between the two. It could be argued that both characters are making the same mistake as Ariel in The *Little Mermaid*. They each come to love the other not through a profound understanding of who they are, but because of the shallow mistaking of another person for the idealized manifestation of their desires. On a surface level, Jasmine and Ariel's motivations seem almost identical, but upon further scrutiny they're really very different. Jasmine is motivated by a desire for freedom, not any particular fascination with the outside world. This is important for understanding why Jasmine loves Aladdin. It isn't because he is a symbol of a more exciting life, it's because he is the first man she's ever met who would refer to her being forced to marry as unfair.

This is the scene on which their relationship is based, and it involves something much deeper than physical infatuation or Lacanian fetishization. The basis of this romantic relationship is a set of shared values. A cliché nugget of advice for lovelorn teenagers is to focus on finding a partner who shares common interests. This is often laughed off as useless advice, and understandably so. After all, a mutual interest in golf or Russian history isn't a sound basis for a love that lasts a lifetime. But this advice is less inane than it first appears. One's interests do more than facilitate activities or topics of conversation. They also say something about what one wants out of life. They can point to a person's core values, a vision of what life is and what should be done with it. If we are lucky enough to find someone who shares that vision, what better basis could there be for a true life partnership?

Of course, Aladdin and Jasmine's relationship still has a long way to go. When they first fall in love, they don't even know each other's names. Not to mention, Jasmine has fled the palace in disguise. Despite this, it isn't until later in the film that the theme of inauthenticity becomes important. Aladdin's disguise as Prince Ali creates two problems for him. The first is overcome fairly quickly during his second encounter with Jasmine. Aladdin, seeing that his royal pretensions only serve to aggravate the Princess, graciously resigns himself to failure out of respect for Jasmine's agency. This surprises and delights Jasmine, and the exchange which follows segues into the film's most romantic musical number. The vocal performance and orchestration make "A Whole New World" truly outstanding, with both perfectly complementing the theme of soaring passion and wonder. The magic carpet ride that the couple share is a truly enchanting experience, and after he and Jasmine return Aladdin states that things are starting to go right for the first time in his life.

Even disregarding his ironic capture by Jafar an instant later, however, it's clear that things aren't really unambiguously going right. After Jafar is exposed as a traitor, Aladdin laments that Prince Ali is to be made Sultan. He feels insecure in his seeming triumph because even though he and Jasmine have both seemingly achieved their goals, their joyful position is predicated on a compromise of their values. Aladdin may have seized an opportunity for a better life, but his maintenance of that life is contingent upon maintaining a deception. Jasmine may have found a husband who respects her and can offer her a life of adventure and freedom, but she is still required to marry a prince and the man she loves could be taken away from her at any time.

Aladdin and Jasmine aren't able to be together openly and honestly until the last scene. Note that even though they become engaged earlier in the film, neither one of them professes love for the other until just before the Genie is freed. When the couple agree to free the Genie rather than use a wish to make Aladdin a prince again, they are taking their mutual love of freedom and giving substance to it in a capacity beyond their own desires. They are making a choice about how they will approach life and the world. They don't just share values, they share a commitment to living their values. Though the Sultan is convinced to change the law by Aladdin's defeat of Jafar, it is symbolically important that he doesn't until after the Genie is free.

The romance between Aladdin and Jasmine falls flat if the film is a simple morality play about authenticity, since the couple is not fully aware of each other's identities until the very end. It also highly devalues Jasmine and the Genie. It reduces Jasmine to Aladdin's reward for learning his lesson, and the Genie's moving struggle for freedom becomes just a side plot. But if the real theme of the movie is freedom, Aladdin and Jasmine are made to be more than just a pair of shallow teenagers who make important life decisions based on physical attraction. They are mature human beings who live their lives together and strive against oppression proudly, with a love based on a deep understanding of the other's core values and a shared vision of the meaning of life. They are quite possibly the most inspiring romantic couple to ever star in a Disney film.

Pocahontas

Pocahontas, along with *The Lion King*, begins what might be called the experimental period of the Disney Renaissance. Emboldened by the runaway success of *Beauty and the Beast* and *Aladdin*, Disney broke away from the Princess formula in the mid-1990s. The films of this era draw from a wide range of history and literature, none of which one would call a fairy tale. Though retroactively labeled a Disney Princess film, *Pocahontas* is obviously meant as a departure from the Princess archetype. The most obvious departure from form is in the film's story, in which the payoff is not the fulfillment of romantic dreams but the prevention of an imminent war.

The film begins in London in the year 1607, where a company of settlers led by veteran adventurer Captain John Smith and greedy politician Governor Ratcliffe commence a sea voyage to find gold in The Americas. Aside from a vicious storm in which John Smith cements his status among the crew by saving the life of a young man named Thomas, the voyage passes without seeming incident. Shortly before the settlers arrive in the New World, the natives of the area rejoice at the return of their chief Powhatan and his warriors from a successful war against another tribe. A warrior named Kocoum is especially honored, and Powhatan plans for the hero to marry his daughter, Pocahontas. Pocahontas herself is highly ambivalent about the proposal, and quite preoccupied with a recurring dream she's been having involving a spinning arrow.

Grandmother Willow, a talking tree who provides Pocahontas with spiritual guidance, believes that the dream has prophetic implications.

Pocahontas and others in her tribe notice the approach of the settlers' ships, and begin to clandestinely observe the newcomers as they begin their excavations and construction projects. Pocahontas specifically observes John Smith, who has been sent by Ratcliffe into the wilderness to scout the area for any native population. The canny Smith becomes aware that Pocahontas is stalking him. He almost shoots her, but holds his fire at the last second because he is captivated by her beauty (or maybe just because she turns out to be a woman). With the help of nature spirits, the two understand each other's language and quickly become friends. They share knowledge of each other's worlds, and Smith gives Pocahontas a compass as a gift. Meanwhile, the warriors observing the main group of settlers are spotted. In a panic, the settlers open fire and one of the warriors is killed. Wary of the danger the settlers represent, Powhatan sends messengers to all the nearby villages with the instruction to send warriors and prepare for an attack on the settlers. After days without finding any gold, Ratcliffe reasons that the natives must have already discovered it and plans to launch an attack against them. The settlers are unsure of whether such an act would be wise, particularly after Smith confesses his friendship with a native. Pocahontas' tribe is also preparing for an attack after the arrival of the neighboring warriors.

Pocahontas and Smith sneak away from their bases to meet with Grandmother Willow. Smith wants to warn Pocahontas of the attack, and Pocahontas hopes she can stop the hostilities by arranging a parley between Smith and her father. Smith is followed by Thomas on instructions from Ratcliffe, and Pocahontas is followed by Kocoum after he is told about Smith by her best friend Nakoma. Smith agrees to Pocahontas' plan and kisses her. In a jealous rage, Kocoum attacks and almost kills Smith. He is shot by Thomas, who flees from the party of warriors that has come looking for Kocoum. The warriors capture Smith, and Powhatan announces that he will be killed at sunrise before the war with the settlers begins. Thomas returns to the settlers with news of Smith's capture, and Ratcliffe uses the men's love for Smith to goad them into an attack.

Pocahontas despairs at her role in the outbreak of hostilities and the capture of the man she loves, but takes heart when she looks at Smith's compass and understands that its needle is the spinning arrow she dreamed of. She rushes to the place where fighting is about the break out, and stops Smith's execution by putting her head above his. Impressed by her courage and wisdom, Powhatan releases Smith and declares peaceful intentions. Realizing that the natives are not hostile, the settlers refuse to fight as well. Ratcliffe, unsatisfied, takes Thomas' gun and tries to shoot Powhatan. Smith jumps in the way of the bullet, and the settlers turn on Ratcliffe. Some of the settlers begin a return voyage to England with a restrained Ratcliffe and a wounded Smith in tow. Pocahontas chooses to stay behind to facilitate harmonious relations between her tribe and the remaining settlers.

Pocahontas is the only Disney film to have true historical events as its (very loose) basis. Sadly, the historical aspects of the film are either highly simplified or utterly fabricated. The actual events surrounding the Jamestown colony and its relationship with Pocahontas' tribe were very complicated and took place over the course of many years. This film features a relationship where instant and implacable suspicion is changed to a lasting peace in less than a week. The film dumbs down actual historical events into a bite-sized parable about the folly of xenophobia, and relies heavily on the use of stereotypes to get its point across. It should be noted that while several characters in this film really existed, they have been so heavily modified to suit the narrative that they might as well be fictional characters, and this analysis will treat them as such.

To the film's credit, it tries to endow both sides of the conflict with some humanity. The natives begin the film just having defeated another tribe, flying in the face of the stereotype of noble savages untouched by the vices of civilization. The film acknowledges that the natives have a civilization of their own, with its own politics and even international relations. The settlers, for their part, are not xenophobic just for the sake of xenophobia. They are simply ignorant and easily manipulated by demagoguery, particularly when their friend is in danger. Both portrayals are not without their problems, however. While the film does an admirable job of examining the settlers' thoughts on the matter of the natives, particularly in one scene where they debate around a campfire the plausibility of the tribe having discovered gold, it seems too easy to put the blame for a long and ugly history of race relations on the powerful few alone. It's true that there have been clarion voices calling for harmony in every time and place, but in a film made largely by white people for a largely white audience Ratcliffe's manipulation of the settlers comes off as an awkward attempt to absolve white guilt. On the other side of the conflict, the natives are idealized to a certain degree. They might not be the inhabitants of paradise, but they are possessed of a certain magical and primitive quality. Their primary method of treating injuries seems to be chanting and shaking turtle shells over the patient. In addition to such oddities, the natives' connection to nature seems to give them access to a functional supernatural force. The scene where the shaman gathers the tribe and reads the magical smoke is entirely gratuitous. The natives learn nothing from the smoke that they don't learn later during their encounter with the settlers.

On the subject of stereotypes, Pocahontas and John Smith are easily the least interesting characters in the film. They have no real personalities of their own, but are rather a conglomeration of gender stereotypes. Compare Smith to the male leads of the two previous films discussed, the Beast and Aladdin. The Beast offers the audience a complex and introspective character, and Aladdin offers a crafty underdog with a heart of gold. Both of these characters have relatable motivations that allow the audience to become invested in their conflicts. Smith isn't so much a relatable character as he is a perfect vehicle for male ego-identification. He's stunningly handsome and adventurous, and these are really his only traits. Smith is said to be an excellent combatant, and appears eager for the opportunity to fight in the beginning of the film. However, none of Smith's supposed combat expertise ever involves itself in the plot except for one scene in which he fatefully gives Thomas the obvious advice of not closing one's eye when firing a gun, but even that has more to do with Thomas' ineptitude than Smith's skill. Smith is an expert warrior for one reason and one reason only: the action hero stereotype demands it.

Pocahontas is largely a collection of gender stereotypes as well. She's indecisive and allows her emotions and intuition to guide her actions completely. She puts an end to the oncoming war between her people and the newcomers not because of any deep understanding of the war's futility or even out of a sense of self-preservation. She stops the war only out of love for John Smith. Even then, she is too indecisive to take concrete action against Smith's execution until his compass points back toward him. The film thinks that it can mask Pocahontas' problematic attributes by painting her with a coat of generic free-spiritedness. The audience is meant to forget that Pocahontas does nothing meaningful of her own volition because she goes off into the wilderness and poses on top of cliffs.

In regards to Pocahontas' posing, she is also sexualized to an uncomfortable degree. In the scene where Smith almost shoots her, there is a long pause before she runs away in which the two stare at each other and the film's romantic motif plays. Smith's reaction actually seems appropriate to the situation. His eyes widen and his mouth hangs open ever so slightly as he gazes upon someone very strange to him and also very beautiful. Pocahontas, on the other hand, appears to have no reaction to him at all. She only stands stoically in the enveloping mist of the waterfall, her chest thrust forward. Her face is completely expressionless, and an extreme close up intimately presents her puffed red lips and her brightly lit bedroom eyes. There's nothing wrong with sex appeal if it makes sense in its own narrative context. John Smith's phenomenal good looks, for example, might be gaudy and indulgent but they don't hurt the story or character in any way. John Smith looks good and he acts accordingly. Pocahontas, on the other hand, doesn't stand impassively in the mists of a waterfall because that's the appropriate reaction to having one's subterfuge discovered. She does it to allow Smith and the audience to be transfixed by her exotic beauty. She is the perfect image of the racial and sexual other.

Smith and Pocahontas, lacking any real personality traits of their own, serve primarily as a representation of their individual sides. They also serve as their side's gender representative. Smith is looked up to by the other settlers, all of whom are men, for his masculine adventurousness. The men themselves are rugged adventurous types, singing about fortune and conquest and swinging weapons as a sign of good fellowship. The only member of the colony who doesn't admire Smith, but rather resents his popularity, is Ratcliffe. While Ratcliffe is a man, his design is rife with ambiguous gender codes. His default costume includes a pink cape and pink bows in his hair. In addition, Ratcliffe is extraordinarily prissy. He wears foppish clothing and keeps his dog perfectly groomed with the help of an ornate bathtub. In addition to these effeminate touches, Ratcliffe appears quite portly in comparison with Smith's athleticism. This last point is important because while the film certainly indulges in the unfortunately common trope of the effeminate villain, it's unlikely that the film is attempting to turn the effeminate traits themselves into something villainous. Rather, Ratcliffe's appearance as a whole is designed to show his contrast from the masculine ideal that Smith represents.

Pocahontas is also heavily contrasted with the oppositely gendered authority figures on her side of the conflict. Throughout the film, Pocahontas mostly relies on the guidance of Grandmother Willow, a female mentor figure that is very rare in Disney films. The only other exception that comes to mind is the Blue Fairy in *Pinocchio*. Even the good fairies in *Sleeping Beauty* serve more as caretakers for Aurora than teachers. Pocahontas seems to be the only one of her tribe who goes to see Grandmother Willow, with the exception of her dead mother, to whom Grandmother Willow apparently served as a mentor as well. One wonders if anyone else in the tribe even knows about Grandmother Willow, and why Pocahontas might be keeping her existence a secret. What is clear is that whatever source the tribe's shaman draws his magic from is not as dedicated to peace and harmony as Grandmother Willow.

The smoke vision of the shaman provides accurate information about the settlers, but presents that information in the most frightening way possible. Thus, the natives adopt a cautious and suspicious approach to the newcomers rather than a friendly and open one. Since the settlers respond to apparent peaceful intentions at the end of the film, it's reasonable to assume that all hostilities could have been avoided if relations had been less suspicious to begin with. The masculine, war-focused magic of the shaman is combined with Kocoum's warrior mentality and Powhatan's vengeful attitude to lay a clear path to war. The hostilities are only averted when Powhatan responds to Pocahontas' calls for harmony and is touched by the feminine magic of nature in the form of multicolored leaves that blow throughout important points in the film.

These magical leaves have feminine associations because of Grandmother Willow and because of some feminine references the natives make to nature such as calling Earth their mother and Pocahontas teaching Smith to see a bear as a mother rather than a beast. It's very possible that the leaves and the wind are even supposed to represent Pocahontas' deceased mother herself. They are first introduced when the shaman mentions that Pocahontas is possessed of the same free spirit as her mother, and Powhatan mentions at one point that he can sometimes feel the presence of his wife when the wind blows. This is possibly foreshadowing for the climactic scene, where Powhatan appears to listen to the magical wind and be calmed by it just before deciding not to kill John Smith. Finally, Pocahontas' mother is known to have had contact with Grandmother Willow, implying a certain heightened spiritual awareness.

Taken together, the gendered sides of the conflict between natives and settlers describe a clear division of labor between the genders by using the foils of the main characters to ascribe a clear set of values to each. The proper place of the masculine, as exemplified by John Smith, is to be bold and adventurous, to be industrious and daring, and to protect those who require it as Smith does when he takes Powhatan's bullet. The place of the feminine, as represented by the influence Pocahontas and the spirits attain over Powhatan, is to domesticate the masculine. The women's role is to calm the anger of the men, and to show them a path to peace and harmony.

Pocahontas at least has a romance that doesn't conclude with an easy happily ever after, as Pocahontas and John Smith are able to draw inspiration and courage from each other without having to give up something important to their way of life. Still, this film has possibly the least called for romance of any Disney movie, and its inclusion cheapens the whole experience. Disney tried to take a step outside the formula of a young woman coming of age to find a fairytale romance, and they failed miserably. The story that Disney decided to tell isn't inspirational, educational, or even entertaining. It's a collection of stereotypes cobbled together with the intent to appear socially aware, but only demonstrating its own inability to deal with any complicated or serious subject matter.

It is well that Disney never attempted to visualize the true passage of history again. Luckily, Disney did not give up in its efforts to make more adult and socially aware films. Their next film, *The Hunchback of Notre Dame*, does a much better job of dealing with the issues of social injustice and the corruption of authority. What's more, the next film provides a fresh new twist on the Disney romance, in which the defining relationship of the film is not between the two protagonists but between the female lead and the film's villain.

The Hunchback of Notre Dame

The Hunchback of Notre Dame is simultaneously one of the grimmest and grandest films Disney has ever produced. Like *Pocahontas*, the film concerns itself primarily with issues of social justice. Unlike *Pocahontas*, which relies on an extraordinarily simplistic story and heavy use of stereotypes, *The Hunchback of Notre Dame* is not afraid to deal honestly with the complexity of the issues it raises. The film's characters, and their feelings toward one another, are deep and rich as well, and while the film is in essence an epic struggle of love against hate, there is far more at stake than the heart of one man. By the end, the film uplifts the audience not only with a vision of love blessed and renewing, but with a vision of a world ennobled and freshly alive.

Set in pre-Reformation France, the film begins with a prologue set 20 years before the beginning of the main story. A group of Romani people (referred to in the film and in the rest of this chapter as Gypsies) attempt to enter the city of Paris in secrecy. They are discovered by the pious and highly bigoted Judge Claude Frollo (who the film is careful to emphasize is not a priest as he is in the original novel). Frollo arrests the Gypsies, but a woman among them flees with a small bundle in her arms. She is pursued by Frollo to the front door of Notre Dame Cathedral. She pleads for sanctuary, but before she can enter the cathedral Frollo snatches the bundle from her and fatally knocks her to the ground. Discovering that the bundle contains a misshapen infant, Frollo attempts to murder him as well. He is stopped at the last moment by Notre Dame's Archdeacon, who chastises Frollo and convinces him to absolve his guilt by caring for the infant. Frollo agrees, but keeps the infant in the cathedral's bell tower.

The child, named Quasimodo by Frollo, grows up in the bell tower and takes up the position of bell ringer. However, his perception of the outside world is warped by Frollo, who teaches him that the corrupt people of Paris will persecute him for his deformity. Fear of this world, and of Frollo, prevents Quasimodo from leaving the tower and attending the annual Festival of Fools for many years. One year, Quasimodo finally ventures out of the tower and attends the festival in disguise. At the same time, a war hero named Captain Phoebus arrives in Paris to take up the post of Captain of the Guard. After rendering assistance to a Gypsy woman named Esmerelda who is being harassed by some guards, Phoebus reports to Frollo at the Palace of Justice. Frollo expresses enthusiasm at Phoebus' war record, and informs him of his plan to rid Paris of the Gypsies by discovering their fabled hiding place, a secret location known as The Court of Miracles. Phoebus believes that Frollo overestimates the threat the Gypsies pose to the city, but for the moment resolves to follow his orders. Music from the town square heralds the start of the festival, and Frollo and Phoebus prepare to attend, as is Frollo's obligation as a public official.

At the festival, where many people are wearing costumes, Quasimodo finds that he is able to wander freely since people assume his hideous face is a mask. Quasimodo enjoys the festival, but is careful to keep out of Frollo's sight. As Frollo takes his place on a stage overlooking the festival, Esmerelda begins a seductive dance for the entertainment of the crowd. Frollo scorns the performance as base and lewd, causing Esmerelda to give him special attention. She dances close to him, gives him a kiss, and pushes his hat down over his face. After the dance, the revelers prepare to crown the King of Fools, a position reserved for the man who can make the ugliest face. Esmerelda pulls Quasimodo up on stage, and it is discovered that his face is not a mask. Having heard rumors of the monstrous bell ringer, the crowd is at first frightened and repulsed. However, the master of ceremonies points out that Quasimodo does indeed have the ugliest face in Paris and deserves the celebrated title of King of Fools.

Quasimodo is thrilled at being not only accepted, but lauded by the townspeople, but the situation changes radically when the guards begin to pelt Quasimodo with foodstuffs. Amused by Quasimodo's plight, the townspeople tie him down and begin to join in his humiliation. Phoebus tries to stop them, but Frollo is furious that Quasimodo disobeyed him by leaving the tower and forbids any assistance. Esmerelda, however, stops the mob and frees Quasimodo in defiance of Frollo. Frollo orders her arrest, but Esmerelda uses trickery to incapacitate and escape the guards. Phoebus notices her sneaking into Notre Dame and follows her. When Phoebus tells Esmeralda that he is unable to arrest her while inside the cathedral, they exchange friendly introductions. Frollo enters the cathedral and orders Phoebus to drag Esmeralda outside and arrest her, but is once again stopped by the Archdeacon. Frollo backs down, but taunts Esmeralda and has guards posted at every entrance to the cathedral.

While trapped inside, Esmeralda makes friends with Quasimodo and helps him to question some of the prejudices instilled in him by Frollo's child-rearing. She helps him understand that Gypsies are not the malicious thieves he believes them to be, and that he himself is not a monster just because of his ugly appearance. Touched by her kindness, Quasimodo helps Esmeralda to escape the cathedral by climbing down the walls. She tries to convince him to come with her to The Court of Miracles, but he refuses her offer. In case he changes his mind, Esmeralda gives him a woven talisman which she says will help him find the Court's location. Meanwhile, Frollo learns of Esmeralda's escape. Driven mad in equal measure by his lust and hatred for Esmeralda, Frollo begins a campaign of terror across the city, arresting Gypsies en masse and offering them money for any information about Esmeralda. Phoebus grows angrier with each arrest made, and finally defies Frollo when ordered to burn down a miller's home with the miller and his family still inside. When Frollo lights the fire himself, Phoebus saves the family but Frollo tries to have him killed. With the help of a disguised Esmeralda, Phoebus manages to escape but is wounded in the process.

Esmeralda takes Phoebus to Quasimodo's tower in hopes of hiding him there. Quasimodo is heartbroken to discover that Esmeralda is in love with Phoebus and not him, but agrees to hide Phoebus until his wound heals. Quasimodo sees Frollo about to enter the cathedral and urges Esmeralda to flee, which she does successfully without being seen. Frollo accuses Quasimodo of helping Esmeralda escape, to which he confesses. Frollo severely admonishes Quasimodo for falling for Esmeralda's supposed

Gypsy trickery, but forgives his error and reassures him that he will do away with Esmeralda soon, as he has discovered the location of The Court of Miracles. Quasimodo and Phoebus decipher Esmeralda's talisman and head for The Court of Miracles to warn the Gypsies, but are followed by Frollo and an overwhelming force of soldiers. Everyone present is imprisoned, and Frollo organizes a public burning for Esmeralda. Quasimodo manages to free her at the last moment and take refuge in Notre Dame. Frollo orders his soldiers to attack the cathedral, and is met with hostile resistance by the townspeople. The attack is successfully repulsed, but Frollo manages to enter the cathedral. He attempts to kill Quasimodo and Esmeralda, but after a dramatic engagement on the roof Frollo himself falls to his death when the stone he stands on crumbles. The fires around the city are put out, and the townspeople gain a new-found acceptance of Quasimodo as they rejoice at Frollo's defeat.

The Hunchback of Notre Dame deals with much more adult themes than is typical of a Disney film, and it is one of the darkest films Disney has ever produced. A dark story doesn't automatically confer quality on a film, but at the very least it represents a daring departure from Disney norms. That said, the film has elements which mark it clearly as Disney's work. The film's aesthetic is possessed of the same smooth line work featured in *Aladdin* and *The Lion King*, and the darkness of the story is generally sanitized. Most tellingly, the film provides a happy ending absent from the original book and most film adaptations. However, just as a dark tone does not guarantee a film's quality, a happy ending doesn't mean that the film is pandering or lazy. The fact of a happy ending matters much less than the implications of that ending. Disney has always been something of a dream factory, a studio which shows the world not as it is but as we might wish it to be. There's no denying that the world of the Disney film is an impressive opiate, but it can also serve as a powerful source of inspiration. This film shows the savagery of oppressive institutions, and then shows the better world that would result if those institutions were overcome. Such a story might come off as foolishly optimistic if such a turn of events were handled in a fairly realistic universe through some easy answer like the power of love, but the characters in this film are only able to resolve the situation though great courage, kindness, and dedication to higher ideals of justice.

One of the most unique elements of the film is its very realistically grounded villain. A far cry from the underwhelming and one-note greedy Ratcliffe, Frollo is at once a perfect personification of oppression and sadism and the most human villain in any Disney film. What makes Frollo so fascinating is that he holds himself to the same outrageous puritanical standards as everyone else, if not higher standards. He might be a hypocrite, but he is genuinely disturbed by his hypocrisy. He does horrible things, but nothing that he can't justify to himself. This is apparent in the way he interacts with both Esmeralda and Quasimodo. Frollo sees Quasimodo as a means to an end, musing as he agrees to adopt him that the infant may be of use to him one day.

Much like Gaston, Frollo has undergone an experience that should have helped him to change for the better, but he fails to learn the proper lesson because of the barriers imposed by his self-image. He feels momentary but intense guilt for the death of

Quasimodo's mother, and even attaches a religious significance to this feeling. The statuary of Notre Dame seems to stare at him, and he feels as though God is judging him most harshly. Rather than questioning the values that brought him to this juncture, however, Frollo instead surmises that Quasimodo was sent to him by God as a sort of helper. He is given the chance to raise a child isolated from the corruption of the outside world, and if he can direct the moral development of this child he will have a loyal ally in his righteous crusade against the Gypsies.

One of the great ambiguities in the film is to what extent Frollo feels fatherly affection towards Quasimodo. There is no doubt of his cruelty to Quasimodo. He belittles his ward at every opportunity. In addition to his frequent references to Quasimodo's monstrous appearance, he often patronizes Quasimodo's intelligence. He sneeringly asks him obvious questions, like whether or not the stone Gargoyles Quasimodo imagines to be his friends are capable of speech. Despite his cruelty, Frollo believes the outside world to be far crueler and does his best to impress this fact upon Quasimodo. When Quasimodo lets slip his desire to go to the festival, Frollo doesn't just chide him for flouting his master's authority. He tries to convince Quasimodo that attending the festival will only result in the scornful condemnation of the sinful townsfolk.

Frollo's view of Paris' citizens is complex. He sees them as corrupt and impious, and yet he claims that his campaign against the Gypsies is on their behalf. The Gypsies, he claims, inspire sin in the citizens by living outside the established social order. Taken together, these attitudes suggest that at least part of

Frollo's prejudice comes from the need for a scapegoat. While at times the townspeople are clearly manipulated by Frollo and his minions, for example when they torment Quasimodo after the guards begin to do so, there is a clear undercurrent of resistance to his authority and Frollo's actions suggest that he is almost as cruel to any seditious elements as he is to the Gypsies. When Phoebus arrives at the Palace of Justice, Frollo is presiding over the whipping of a man implied to be his previous captain of the guard. When Esmeralda defies Frollo at the festival, she seems to have the support of the very crowd that was tormenting Quasimodo only a moment ago.

In his constant failure to be self-critical, Frollo concludes that the citizens' failure to be brought to heel by his authoritarian regime must be the result of a malignant external influence. Frollo himself becomes an example of this principle when he is tempted by Esmeralda. Unable to accept his own sexuality, he engages in textbook victim blaming behavior and concludes that Esmeralda is cunningly seducing him in a deliberate attempt to undermine his moral authority. An overly simplistic reading of the film might suggest that Frollo's destructive oppression of those around him stems entirely from his self-imposed celibacy. It would be more accurate to describe Frollo as a representation of patriarchal principles, a vindictive old man seeking to at once exploit female sexuality for his own purposes and denigrate it as disruptive and immoral.

The film might seem to be guilty of the same paradigm in certain scenes. After all, Esmeralda's erotic dance number at the festival could be read as a form of provocation. There are two important things to keep in mind before jumping to these conclusions. First of all, in every scene afterward, Frollo is clearly shown to be the sexual aggressor. Secondly, while Esmeralda does pay particular attention to Frollo during the dance, she does so as a means of exposing his hypocrisy rather than as an attempt at seduction. The film makes it clear that Frollo is the one at fault in this scenario. Esmeralda's sexuality is not presented as a justification for Frollo's actions, but as a progressive force that exists in opposition to Frollo's repressive tyranny.

Esmeralda's progressive nature extends beyond her liberated sexuality. She is the archetypal example of a strong and active female character. She is victimized by society, for her gender and for her ethnicity, but she doesn't allow herself to be defined as a victim. She evades oppressive power structures when it is pragmatic to do so, but isn't afraid to stand up for what's right if the situation calls for it. When the guards attempt to steal the money she earns in a street performance, her first priority is to escape them. Failing to do so, she doesn't miss an opportunity to defy them, insinuating their own corruption and criminality.

Perhaps the most important thing about Esmeralda as a progressive entity is that she has the capacity to view her oppression in a broad context. While taking shelter in Notre Dame, she muses that her guile and performing talents grant her advantages not enjoyed by other Gypsies. She's even able to extend this empathy to other oppressed groups, citing the persecution of Quasimodo and her people as two symptoms of a greater injustice. Though Quasimodo is technically of Gypsy ethnicity, he has grown up in isolation from Gypsy culture and doesn't occupy the same social space as them. Esmeralda's ability to empathize with the plight of others sets her in stark contrast to Pocahontas, who only solved a larger social problem for her own benefit and that of one man. Esmeralda is committed to a better world for all and yet is unfettered by the expectations of others. Her will to do what is right is not dependent on the affections of Phoebus or Quasimodo, she merely shares with them her transforming vision of a just society. It's true that Esmeralda does serve as an object of competition between the male characters of the film, and it's true that the resolution of the film's conflict depends mainly on Quasimodo's moral development, but Esmeralda remains a steadfast and helpful companion to the men in the film, and not merely someone to be protected. Indeed, she rescues Phoebus and Quasimodo at least as often as they rescue her.

The Hunchback of Notre Dame is notable among Disney films for building up a potential romance for the protagonist but pointedly not having it go anywhere. Yet, the romance is not gratuitous. It's important to Quasimodo's character development to show that neither his sense of right and wrong nor his self-worth are predicated on the romantic affections of Esmeralda. Of course Quasimodo is disappointed to find that his affections are not returned, and he even makes a show of considering giving up on helping her. Just after Frollo threatens to attack the Court of Miracles, Phoebus entreats Quasimodo to help him warn the Gypsies. Quasimodo refuses at first, and briefly reflects on the possibility that Frollo was right all along. Maybe his ugliness does preclude him from genuine friendship. Maybe Esmeralda has been deceiving him for her own gain all along. This consideration is only momentary, however, and it's hard to tell if Quasimodo even believes it himself. Whether his surrender is at all genuine or not, he quickly realizes that even if Esmeralda is not in love with him she has been a better friend to him than Frollo ever was.

As with many of Disney's protagonists, Quasimodo's moral turning point might be inspired by romantic love, but what truly transforms him is the opportunity to see the world from a broader perspective. The kindness Esmeralda showed him proves that Frollo's worldview is wrong. Not only can Quasimodo see that people in general are much less corrupt than Frollo makes them out to be, but he is finally able to see himself through the eyes of people who see him as something other than a monster. Phoebus fills this role for Quasimodo as well as Esmeralda. He doesn't command Quasimodo to come with him to warn Esmeralda, he appeals to him. He tells Quasimodo to do what he thinks is right, and even if this phrase is dismissive and judgmental he is endowing Quasimodo with moral agency. He gives Quasimodo his first real chance for introspection. Quasimodo is at last forced to put aside Frollo's dogma and his own self-doubt and ask himself what he thinks is right. Quasimodo undergoes a paradigm shift, in which he ceases to fight for Esmeralda (which is by extension a fight for his own gratification) and instead fights against Frollo's evil. He becomes a fuller person as a result, and unabashedly supports Esmeralda and Phoebus' union by the end of the film.

The film's take on romance is that there is a sense of right and wrong that transcends it, and that romantic failure or success doesn't have to be anyone's defining characteristic. Whether a person has the courage and kindness to stand up for what is right is more important than whether their ordeal results in a storybook marriage. Quasimodo's respect for Esmeralda and Phoebus' love sets him in direct contrast with Frollo, and shows that people are more than their upbringing. The film echoes a sentiment expressed in *Beauty and the Beast*, that often the most monstrous are those who do not appear as such. What makes a monster is a lack of care for others, an inability to see one's fellow humans as anything more than minions or threats. Frollo is just the sort of monster which besets the real world, a madman who ascribes his earthly power to his own righteousness.

Just as in the real world, in *The Hunchback of Notre Dame* it takes all kinds of people working together to stop such monsters. Those oppressed must find the courage to speak out against injustice. Those who serve the institutions from which monsters draw their power must be uncompromising in their desire to rid the world of corruption, and come to understand that the society they serve is not invulnerable to abuses. Finally, those who have lived their lives raised in the shadows of monsters must be shown the richness and essential worth of the world they have only observed from on high. They must learn that there is a better way to live than to be engulfed by fear of themselves and those around them, and see that the monsters which profess to protect them have made them into pawns.

The comprehension of all these courageous truths begins with the understanding that none of us stand alone. Esmeralda, unable to find justice on her own, finds an unlikely ally in the captain of the guard. Quasimodo finds kindness in the hearts of those he has been taught his whole life to fear. Romantic love, one of the strongest bonds between people, plays a part in this great unification, of course. Such love, however, is only one part of a greater dream.

Hercules

Hercules, like *The Hunchback of Notre Dame*, is a film which stands apart from the rest of the Disney library. The visual style of the film is absolutely unique, and the characters are also fresh for a Disney film, despite similar characters being fairly common in movies and television. Perhaps befitting the mythical and archetypal nature of the ancient source material, the film has the most straightforward character arc of any Disney film.

After being turned mortal and stolen from Mount Olympus as a baby, Hercules is on a quest to attain godhood by becoming a hero. After training with Phil the satyr, he heads for the city of Thebes in hopes of finding monsters or disasters to fight. On the way, he saves a woman named Megara (Meg) from a centaur she had been trying to recruit for an uprising against the gods led by Hades, God of the Underworld. Thus, Hercules is brought to the attention of Hades. Hades had previously engineered Hercules' kidnapping and believed him to be dead. Intent on killing Hercules before his 18th birthday, so as to prevent the fulfillment of a prophecy foretelling his defeat by the young hero, Hades sends monsters to fight Hercules, but only succeeds in increasing his fame.

Hoping to find a weakness in Hercules, Hades sends Meg to ascertain one using a date as a cover. Much to her surprise, Meg discovers that she has fallen in love with Hercules despite having had a bad relationship in the past that ended in Hades owning her soul. Meg refuses to cooperate with Hades, but he uses her to trick

Hercules into giving up his strength for a day on the condition that she remain unharmed. As Hades begins his takeover of Olympus with the help of the Titans, a Cyclops attacks Thebes. Despite his weakened state, Hercules is able to kill the monster, but Meg is mortally wounded in the process. Hercules' strength is restored, and he is able to defeat Hades and the Titans. After the battle, he travels to the Underworld to rescue Meg from death by taking her place. This act of self-sacrifice makes him a true hero, and thus he is saved from death, but he chooses to remain mortal with Meg rather than become a god. Apparently someone forgot to tell Hercules that romance between mortals and gods is not unusual in Greek legends.

The overall tone of the film could best be described as the classical juxtaposed with the modern. This tone is set right from the opening scene of the film. As the camera moves among realistically rendered Greek statues, a deep voice provides dramatic narration about the grandeur of classical heroes. The scene culminates with a slow push in on a pot which features a classical black figure rendering of Hercules fighting a lion. In a deliberate contrast of reserve and energy, the camera quickly pushes in on the Muses who complain about the narrator's overly serious presentation and take over narrating duties. They are drawn with the same surreal style as the other characters in the film, and instead of dry dramatic speech they narrate almost entirely in soul music interludes.

The thread of modernity runs through the whole film. Thebes is fairly directly presented as a classical Greek New York City, right down to the nickname "The Big Olive." Hades fits into this atmosphere perfectly. James Woods' performance doesn't convey the profundity one might expect from a god, but instead the sense of a smarmy fast talker perfectly at home in an episode of *Seinfeld*. The film also makes liberal use of pop culture references. Examples include a large mosaic in Thebes that advertises Hercules merchandise and mimics Michael Jordan's line of sneakers, and Hades' use of *I Love Lucy* references while in the process of becoming the master of the cosmos. Such moments are no doubt influenced by the popularity of the Genie in *Aladdin*. It can hardly be a coincidence that *Hercules* features a famous comedian in the role of a large blue man with supernatural powers and anachronistic speech patterns.

The modernity of the story goes beyond the reimagining of the Hercules myth with pop culture elements; it is also reflected in the values of the story. The Greek gods are present in this film as aspects of a good vs. evil cosmic dualism rather than as the embodiment of morally null natural forces. The modern ideology of this film is perhaps best illustrated by Hercules' self-sacrifice, and the presentation of compassion and love as the truest expression of heroism. Such a moral is radically different from the source material, in which Hercules proved himself worthy of immortality through his cunning and determination. Hercules, like the gods themselves, has been transformed in this film from someone who is morally null into a paragon of modern goodness. The mythical Hercules is not totally without nobility, but his sense of morality is very disconnected from a modern audience's ideas of heroism. He does endeavor to atone for the deaths of his wife and children, but going on adventures to kill monsters and win the favor of a king hardly seems the obvious method of atoning for such a deed to the modern mind.

Disney's *Hercules* replaces this dark quest for atonement with a coming of age story, which is much more palatable to a modern audience and much more typical of Disney films. After setting up the film's plot while Hercules is still a baby, the film shows him as an awkward teenager. His goal is to find acceptance in society. He hopes to achieve this by becoming stronger and battling monsters. He also puts a great deal of emphasis on saving people, particularly damsels in distress. His first attempt at the rescue of such a person introduces him to Meg, who is by far the most interesting and ambiguous character in the film. Most of the other characters are very straightforward. Hercules is the archetypal strong and innocent protagonist. Hades is the conniving and jealous brother obsessed with power. Pegasus is the goofy animal sidekick. Meg is a little harder to pin down, particularly for a lead Disney female.

The sticking point of Meg's ambiguity is that she begins the film as Hades' minion, but ends the film as Hercules' girlfriend. She fills the odd narrative niche of being both an obstacle and a reward for Hercules. It's hard to deny that Meg does the right thing by abandoning her service to Hades, but it's also important to ask what her new relationship with Hercules represents. Is she a woman who rediscovers the happiness she lost long ago through her love for a wonderful man, or is she a lost soul who needs to have the sarcasm and frigidity "tamed" out of her by a man worthy of her love? It's fairly obvious that the film intends for her character arc to be read in the former way, and it might even seem like a stretch to interpret it the latter way. To explain how such an interpretation is even feasible, this chapter will to refer once again to the work of Laura Mulvey.

Despite Mulvey's rather insightful comments on the visual pleasures of film and the sexual division of labor with regard to those pleasures, she says a lot of things about the role of women in film that simply don't apply to film in general. Many of her ideas apply specifically to crime and horror films. She seems to have a particular fascination with the work of Alfred Hitchcock, citing examples from such classics as *Rear Window* and *Vertigo*. At this point, the obvious question is what Hercules has to do with such movies. Obviously, the overall genre of the film is quite different. Hercules and Phil seem to be right out of a standard sports film. However, one of the film's trademarks is copious cross pollination among genres. Whether such an odd juxtaposition of genres and tropes creates a confused mishmash or a unique entertainment experience is up to individual taste, but in the middle of all this it doesn't seem at all out of place that Meg plays very much into the familiar role of the noir femme fatale. She seduces the hero in an attempt to further her own agenda, but finds herself succumbing to his charm by the end of the film.

On the subject of seduction, Meg is also the most overtly sexualized woman in any Disney film. Yes, Ariel might engage in a few questionable poses during her main musical number and Esmeralda's dancing obliquely alludes to striptease, but Hades makes explicit references to Meg's sexual attributes and her seduction of Hercules is exactly that, a seduction. It involves a great deal of innuendo and aggressive body language. Sexuality in and of itself isn't problematic or demeaning, in fact the free expression of sexuality can be a profoundly liberating experience. Everything depends on context, and Meg's situation fits Mulvey's outline of sexuality in crime films disturbingly well.

So what exactly does Mulvey say about female sexuality in crime films? As stated previously, her argument is largely predicated upon phallocentric Freudian psychology. As described by Mulvey, the patriarchal social order casts the female as a dangerous other to the masculine by accentuating the fear of castration she inspires through her lack of a penis. At the same time, women are an essential part of this social order. The other that they are made into gives men a mechanism of self-identification. In simple terms, men know they are men because they are not women. An excellent example of this is the sexual division of labor common in film. Male characters propel the story forward through action and power, thus serving as a point of ego identification. Females serve as an object of voyeuristic pleasure and a gratuitous distraction from the narrative at hand rather than contributing in any meaningful regard. Much as this division of labor results from an attempt to reconcile the two visual pleasures of film, the classic femme fatale is a reconciliation of the tension between the pleasures the female form evokes in the male gaze and the anxiety that the female genitals evoke in the masculine castration complex.

The femme fatale is a controversial figure in cinema because she seems to defy the patriarchy though her overt sexuality and moral agency, but she often ends the film in some form of submission to it. A femme fatale, at least in most seminal works of film noir, almost always ends up dead or incarcerated. Alternatively, she may simply submit to the hero's masculine authority and adopt a more conventional lifestyle. Whatever her eventual fate, it is always a result of her being acted upon by the hero. She is usually opposed to the hero in some way, but comes to him in the guise of an ally. The hero is won over by her wiles, but either doggedly pursues any evidence of traitorous intent or is compelling enough to the femme fatale to induce her to confess her own duplicitous intentions. As a result, she is exposed and punished. In this way, the hero and the audience are able to eat their cake and have it too. They are able to indulge in the sexual image of the cinematic woman, and also assuage their castration anxiety by painting that same sexuality as transgressive and controllable.

If all this talk of castration anxiety and transgressive sexuality seems a little abstract, perhaps using Meg as a case study will make this principle a little more concrete. Right from the beginning, Meg is shown to be a disruption. When Hercules spots her being menaced by a centaur, he becomes angry on her behalf and acts without properly analyzing the situation first. Such a course of action runs contrary to his training, as Phil points out. Such an error could be (and is) chalked up to Hercules' inexperience. He is, after all, rescuing a damsel for the first time. Still, Phil does blame Meg for Hercules' blunder. He tells Hercules not to let feminine beauty distract him during future heroic endeavors. As Hercules ignores Phil completely in favor of pursuing a flirtatious conversation with Meg, Phil and Hercules' equine companion Pegasus become increasingly annoyed with her. Phil continues to have professional concerns about her effect on Hercules, shifting the blame for Hercules' failings onto Meg. Pegasus' reasons for disliking Meg are more mystifying. He appears to be jealous of Hercules' infatuation for her. Of course, Pegasus is not presented as any kind of romantic rival for Meg. His anger is motivated by the threat she represents to the integrity of his masculine social group. Such an irrational sentiment is not uncommon in film. Many romantic comedies feature the male lead's friends strongly advising him not to pursue the female lead and describing her as trouble. This idea is even present in other Disney films, including *The Jungle Book* and *The Lion King*.

Hercules' companions continue to dislike Meg for most of the film. After Meg's date with Hercules, just as the two are about to kiss, Phil and Pegasus arrive and take Hercules back to his training grounds. Faced with Phil's outrage, Meg attempts to assuage him by admitting that Hercules missing his obligations for the afternoon was her fault. While she was the one that proposed the date, such a statement ignores that Hercules had to choose to accept her proposition. For Meg to say that the situation is her fault implies that it is her responsibility not to tempt Hercules, and transforms her sexuality into a locus of guilt. Of course, in the context of the story, Meg is guilty. She is manipulating Hercules to discover any weakness he might have. The problem isn't that Meg feels guilty about betraying someone who is so kind to her and helping the god of death overthrow the natural order. The problem of Meg's sexuality being bound up with malicious intent exists on a more metafictional level.

To illustrate this point, compare Meg with Aladdin, another Disney character who pursues a romantic relationship under false pretenses. When Aladdin disguises his identity to pursue Jasmine, the situation is framed as a necessary evil. Aladdin has no malicious intent, his subterfuge is just the only way to circumvent the social structure that prevents both him and Jasmine from being with the person they love. When Meg, a femme fatale, deceives her romantic partner, it is with the express intent of his violent defeat.

Phil discovers Meg talking to Hades while defying him. He misinterprets her sarcasm as a genuine desire to kill Hercules, and his warning to Hercules that she cannot be trusted causes Hercules to violently lash out. Once again, Meg is an agent of disturbance. This time, she has led to the complete breakdown of Phil's friendship with Hercules. Despite Meg's defiance of Hades, she still provides the means to Hercules' downfall when Hades offers him Meg's freedom in exchange for his strength. Only afterwards does Hades reveal that Meg was working for him when she pursued Hercules. Hercules is understandably crestfallen. In fact, he is so hurt by Meg's betrayal that he engages in a suicidal attack upon the Cyclops destroying Thebes. Admittedly, he doesn't say this outright. He says only that there are worse things than dying. He could simply feel compelled to help the city, or he could be afraid of being thought a coward. However, his tone of voice seems to indicate that he has personally experienced worse things than death, such as Meg's betrayal. Also, he appears dismissive of Meg, pushing her out of the way, and in a later scene gesturing toward her while commenting on the futility of dreams.

Meg, unable to convince Hercules not to fight, decides to help him by finding his friends, a labor to repair the male social group. First, she rescues Pegasus, who has previously been captured by

Hades' impish minions Pain and Panic. The henchmen had lured Pegasus away from the training grounds by disguising themselves as a seductive female flying horse, an obvious parallel to Hercules' own situation. Together, Meg and Pegasus find Phil, who is about to leave on a boat back to his home island. Meg is made to confess her wrongdoing and induces Phil to return to Hercules by saying his friend will die without his help. Phil motivates Hercules to fight back and kill the Cyclops, but when the monster stumbles off a cliff the impact causes a column to collapse. Before it can fall on Hercules, Meg pushes him out of the way. As a result of her mortal injury, Hades' deal with Hercules becomes invalid and Hercules gets his strength back.

This act of self-sacrifice parallels Hercules' own selfless act at the end of the film, and it also serves as Meg's ultimate act of redemption. It is here too that Meg confesses her love for Hercules, a suitable culmination to the increased emotional vulnerability she has exhibited since Hades revealed her former allegiance. Thus, the femme fatale arc is complete. The woman's sexual manipulation has compromised the male hero, and she has been exposed and brought low herself to give the hero status through her defeat. Still, Meg's story is not over. Unlike most characters in her role, Meg endures both potential fates of the repentant femme fatale. She is killed defending the man she sought to manipulate, and after a rescue from the Underworld she is able to settle down with him as well.

Such a critical reading of *Hercules* might make the film seem highly problematic, but it's important to remember that for all the patriarchal assumptions that go into her arc Meg is still a very positive character in many ways. Like all femme fatales, her unapologetic sexuality combined with her self-assurance is highly subversive to patriarchal mores. More importantly, Meg is very unlike most such characters in that even after her wrongdoing is exposed she maintains much of her original persona. After telling Hercules she loves him, she makes an endearingly sarcastic remark that calls back to her first encounter with him, and as the two kiss on Mount Olympus she grabs her new lover with aggressive passion. It's fairly clear that just because she's found a new boyfriend doesn't mean Meg is about to become a dainty and fawning princess like so many other Disney women.

Meg represents a radical revision of the Disney romance formula. Her relationship with Hercules might fit the happily ever after bill fairly well, but Meg has had a bad romantic relationship before the movie begins. Meg sold her soul to save her previous boyfriend, only to have him betray her for another woman. For a Disney movie to admit that romantic love might not last forever is a pretty big deal. This point of character development also makes her much more sympathetic than other femme fatales, who usually act out of greed. Meg's reaction to this bad breakup is also handled very well. Bitterness toward men was a fairly common cliché in films of the 1990s, but given the gravity of the betrayal Meg went through, it certainly seems justified. Jasmine might have resisted being forced to marry, but Meg is the only Disney romantic lead to be resistant to the very idea of love. Meg has to go through a lot of hardship to find a fulfilling relationship, and it is impossible to deny that her new love gives her the courage to stand up to someone who just wants to use her and ultimately leads to a life of happiness and a renewed faith in humanity. To read Meg's relationship with Hercules purely as an exercise in patriarchal symbolism denies all that she and Hercules gain by finding each other.

So, is Meg a progressive character who adds complexity and moral agency to the classic Disney heroine, or is she simply a formulaic and problematic depiction of women transferred from another genre into a Disney film? There is no easy answer to that question, and it is that very ambiguity between subversion and acquiescence that makes Meg such a fascinating character. One thing is certain: Meg will never be an official Disney Princess. She doesn't have the innocence and unambiguously delightful persona required to be featured in Disney's most successful marketing campaign. Meg is a clear illustration of the fact that Disney films are much more nuanced than the image the company presents in its marketing. This fact will be even better illustrated by the next chapter, which discusses Mulan, a character who does enjoy the official title of Disney Princess, but is even further removed from other bearers of that title than Pocahontas.

Mulan

Mulan is by and large the great exception when it comes to Disney films. For one thing, it's the only Disney film which could be considered a war movie. The more talked about exception is that it features a Princess who fights. Of course, despite being one of the official Disney Princesses from the very beginning of the campaign, Mulan isn't actually a princess. She doesn't even marry a prince, and her romance (in true war movie fashion) is highly tangential to the main story. These factors might make Mulan seem out of place in this book, but Mulan deals more overtly (and yet subtly and artfully) with questions of gender than any other Disney film. As such, this film is often regarded as Disney's most self-critical film prior to their parodic phase. It would seem remiss not to analyze the Disney heroine who strays farthest from feminine stereotypes and still remains an important part of the studio's image.

Set in medieval China, the film begins with an invasion by a horde of Huns led by a war chief named Shan Yu, who is eager to prove the strength of his person and his army by conquering the Emperor. As the Emperor sets plans in motion to raise an army for a counter-attack, a young woman named Fa Mulan begins preparations to meet her town's matchmaker and bring her family honor by marrying a suitable husband. Given Mulan's clumsiness and poor head for rules and sayings, neither she nor her family are confident in her ability to make a good impression. Due to a set of madcap circumstances involving a cricket and some black ink, Mulan ends up setting the matchmaker on fire, drenching her with hot tea, and ruining her makeup. As Mulan laments her inability to fulfill her duties to society and her family, the Emperor's counselor Chi Fu arrives and hands out conscription notices to one man in every family in town. Being the only man in the Fa family, it falls to Mulan's aged and ailing father to fight the Huns.

Despite strenuous objection from Mulan, her father is determined to fulfill his obligation to the Emperor for honor's sake. Knowing that her father would never survive a battle, Mulan steals his sword and armor and runs away to join the army in his place disguised as a young man named Fa Ping. She is accompanied by Mu Shu, a miniature dragon who lost the trust of the Fa family ancestors some time ago and is determined to regain his standing by making Mulan a war hero. His contributions to the plot are mainly setting off pyrotechnics and serving as a Jiminy Cricket-like conscience figure for Mulan. At first, Mulan has a hard time getting along with her comrades and her lack of physical strength proves a handicap. She is almost discharged by her commanding officer, Captain Li Shang, but wins his respect and that of the other soldiers when she uses her cleverness to complete a training exercise none of the other soldiers had finished wherein she retrieves an arrow from the top of a tall pole. She accomplishes this by wrapping the weights intended to hinder her around the pole as a sort of climbing anchor.

Eager for Mulan to prove her courage in battle, Mu Shu forges an urgent message from General Li, Shang's father. The troops move out to the village where the General is stationed, only to find it and the army completely destroyed by the Huns. Shang presses them onward into the Tung Shao pass to catch up with the Huns before they reach the Imperial City and the Emperor. The troops are later ambushed by the Huns. Their pyrotechnic cannons are sufficient to subdue the initial assault, but it soon becomes clear that they are no match for the horde's sheer numbers. Resigned to the defeat of his men, Shang orders the one remaining cannon to be fired at Shan Yu in a final gesture of revenge. At the last moment, Mulan sees an opportunity and makes off with the cannon. Charging toward the horde, she fires the cannon at a nearby mountainside just as Shan Yu reaches her. The resulting avalanche buries the Huns, but Shan Yu manages to wound Mulan with his sword. While Mulan is being treated, her womanhood is discovered. Shang refuses to execute her out of gratitude for single-handedly defeating the Huns and saving his life, but he and the rest of the army abandon her on the mountainside while they march to the Imperial City. As Mulan reflects on her failure and prepares to face her dishonored family, she observes Shan Yu and a few of his best soldiers emerging from the snow and heading for the city.

Mulan tries to warn the soldiers that the Huns are alive, but no one believes her until the Emperor is captured and his palace closed off. Mulan concocts a plan for her and her companions to sneak into the palace disguised as concubines, subdue Shan Yu's men, and create an opening for Shang to rescue the Emperor. The plan works, but Shang and Mulan are trapped with a very angry Shan Yu, who chases Mulan through the palace. In a display of cunning, Mulan manages to disarm him and lure him into an explosive trap. Having saved the Emperor, Mulan is publicly acknowledged as a hero and returns home to her family with the gifts the Emperor has given her. Mu Shu is reinstated as a Fa family guardian by the ancestors, and it is heavily implied that Mulan pursues a romantic relationship with Shang.

Mulan is Disney's most obvious example of a "strong female character." The tendency to convey strength in women as combat ability is natural enough, since the role of a savvy combatant is one that has traditionally been closed off to women, but such a notion of strength fails to examine the assumptions behind the value that our culture places on combat in the first place. Mulan's courage, cunning and loyalty make her an excellent role model, but it's worth remembering that a progressive portrayal of women need not involve violence. Indeed, arguments could be made which call Mulan's progressiveness into question. After all, she does ostensibly go to war for the sake of a man, and seems to have internalized her oppression to a degree. When she is discovered, she only apologizes. She doesn't dispute the justice of the law which forbids her to serve in the army, which she would be in an excellent position to do given the fact that she just defeated an entire army by herself. Earlier in the film, she laments of her inability to marry rather than resenting her obligation to marry, as Jasmine did. All of these facts might cast doubt in the minds of some as to Mulan's credibility as a strong and independent role model, but if one examines the subtleties behind these facts one can discern a message about gender much more intricate and universal than the supposed feminist message for which the movie is known.

To begin its study of gender roles, the film's first order of business is to almost entirely exclude sexuality from the equation.

After taking a step back from the sexual undertones of *The Little Mermaid*, it seems that Disney films get more sexual up until *Hercules*. *Aladdin* has Jasmine's dress and its vaguely erotic connotations, *Hunchback of Notre Dame* has Esmerelda pole dancing, and *Hercules* has Megara as the voluptuous locus of sexual danger that Laura Mulvey is so fascinated with. *Mulan*, by contrast, takes almost every opportunity to avoid sexualizing its characters.

Mulan spends the majority of the movie in very practical armor, and the film tactfully declines to exploit the two occasions when she actually bathes naked. There are no tantalizing shots of her silhouetted body, except one where she's behind a screen. Even then, her silhouette is awkwardly falling into the bath, not languidly sliding into it. Mulan's nudity is a plot point in the second bathing scene, where her comrades come dangerously close to discovering her secret. This is probably one of the only scenes in cinema history where the nudity of a beautiful woman is played for comedy rather than sex appeal. The only character in the film who is sexualized at all is Shang, who appears before his soldiers on the first day of training shirtless and very buff. Even this token display is mocked. When asked by Shang to retrieve an arrow from the top of a pole, a tough and sarcastic soldier named Yao mutters under his breath, "I'll get that arrow, pretty boy, and I'll do it with my shirt on."

A crucial observation regarding Mulan is that she adopts a male persona not out of principle but out of practicality. Her ostensible reason for going to war is to protect her father, but she confesses to Mu Shu at the start of the third act that her true motivation was to explore the possibility that her talents might be better suited to a military life than the one prescribed for her by society. Even without this dialogue, it's clear that Mulan finds some personal fulfillment by being in the army. If she didn't, Shang's dismissal during the struggles with her training would have been a perfect opportunity to return home without going into a dangerous combat situation. The film passes up an opportunity to broadly criticize the role of women in medieval China by having Mulan genuinely lament her inability to fulfill it. This may seem an odd choice, given that such a criticism would be welcomed by modern viewers. The film, however, chooses to maintain fidelity to its own characters and world by having Mulan and all the other women in the film be invested in the system as it is. None of the rituals or norms of Mulan's society are presented as harmful in and of themselves. They only become problematic because Mulan's worth as a person in the eyes of society hinges upon her ability to conform to the gender norms of obedience and idle beauty.

This isn't a case of Disney easing up in its criticism of the gendered system of the film's world, or implicitly condoning the restriction of women's right to self-determination. This is Disney showing exactly what is wrong with a system that requires women to be demure and passive and men to project an image of strength even if they are barely able to walk without the assistance of a cane. Such a system isn't destructive just because a film says so. It is destructive because people unable to live up to society's expectations are shunned and disgraced, or else simply die. Beyond Mulan's ineptitude at the traditional duties of a woman, the film drives this point home by showcasing the dichotomy between one's private and public persona. When Mulan is first introduced, she is memorizing various feminine virtues to prepare for her meeting with the matchmaker. These virtues include delicacy, politeness, and poise among other things. The irony of the situation is that Mulan is stating these virtues out loud while chewing a mouthful of rice. There's nothing truly scandalous about this contrast, but it subtly and concretely establishes that the image Mulan is presenting to society is dissonant with her private self.

This dissonance forms the basis of Mulan's only solo musical number, in which she ponders the inauthentic image she must present to the world. The crisis of identity which this song embodies is the crux of Mulan's character. Having failed at playing the part of a woman in society, she joins the army reasoning that she might succeed in the male role. Given the binary between male and female that Mulan has been conditioned to see in the world, such a change of pace seems only logical. However, Mulan doesn't succeed at embodying masculine stereotypes any more than she does at playing into feminine ones. When she comes to the camp, she tries to blend in and fails hilariously. She tries to act tough and ends up starting a brawl that engulfs the camp. She tries to act slovenly and is called a lunatic.

Mulan's failure at masculinity isn't just a moment of comic relief, it extends into the training montage that is one of the film's highlights. The virtues of masculinity are listed in this song's chorus, one of the most stirring in all of Disney's music. "You must be swift as the coursing river, with all the force of a great typhoon, with all the strength of a raging fire, mysterious as the dark side of the moon." In all the excitement of the song, it's easy to forget that Mulan doesn't actually possess any of these virtues. Her ability doesn't lie in her physical strength, but in her cleverness and tactical sensibilities. She is able to retrieve Shang's arrow from the top of the pole because she is able to use the straps around the weights she has to carry to her advantage, not because of sheer physical ability. Of course Mulan's strength and endurance grow over time, but these moments are just glossed over in the montage. Mulan's display of her intelligence and determination is what really serves as a turning point. Not only does it gain her the respect of Shang, it apparently gives her the drive to succeed in her training.

The point is that Mulan doesn't succeed by embracing one set of stereotypes or the other. She succeeds, both in her training and in actual battle, through those traits which are most essential to her identity irrelevant of gender. Note that she demonstrates her wit early on by helping an old man win a board game on her way to the matchmaker. Her intelligence is present whether she is trying to fulfill a masculine or feminine role. One visual cue that ties the beginning and end of the film to this theme beautifully is Mulan's use of a fan. In an early scene, she tries to use it to put out the embers on the matchmakers dress and only fans the flames. In the climax, she uses a fan to disarm Shan Yu in preparation for his imminent immolation. A feminine object, when restricted to its intended purpose, proves worse than useless. When Mulan has expanded her perspective enough to transcend gender and rely on her own wit above all else, she finds a new use for an old feminine accoutrement.

This theme is implicit in the musical construction of *Mulan*. The film features one song that succinctly outlines the expectations upon women and features lyrical and delicate harmonies, and one song that brings masculinity to the fore and features a hard militaristic drumbeat and a booming choir as its musical base. The visuals complement the masculine/feminine dichotomy as well. The first song features comparatively long takes and slow, sweeping camera movements as if to suggest poised dancing, the flow of Mulan's dresses, or the elegant movements of her makeup brush. The latter song is a rapid-fire succession of quick and violent images. An exploding tent, a face smashed against a stone block.

The montage only slows down twice. Once is when Mulan stumbles and falls while carrying a pair of heavy bags, Shang takes the bags from her, and she is humiliated by her weakness. Mulan can't keep up with the rest of the soldiers, and the pace of these few shots isn't keeping up with the rest of the montage. The slow section of the sequence continues in the scene where Mulan retrieves the arrow. This reflects her problem solving process. She slows down and analyses the situation. She doesn't try to just rush through it, or the montage, like she and the other soldiers had before. In an instance of moderate cleverness, the aesthetics of one song and the music of another are brought together in a brief reprise of "Make a Man out of You" as Mulan's comrades don makeup and dresses in preparation for sneaking into the palace at the beginning of the film's climax. This comes after the kidnapping of the Emperor has exonerated Mulan and her comrades have learned to put aside gender stereotypes and trust her as they did when they thought she was a man.

In between these two songs is the song where Mulan contemplates her role in life and how to reconcile it with her own self. This is compositionally the simplest song in the film. Its most elaborate feature is a few bridges reminiscent of traditional Chinese music. The song is also shot simply, consisting of basic medium shots with the occasional medium close-up. These shot types are among the most basic in film. Over the course of the song, Mulan removes the makeup and accessories she adopted in the previous sequence, and the camera complements this by presenting an image of Mulan which is largely unadorned as well. The music and the visuals communicate that Mulan is shown here as the most essential representation of herself, and the message of the song is universal. It's easy to imagine any young person, woman or man, struggling with their identity in the face of societal expectations. The message of this song, and the song "True to Your Heart" that plays over the closing credits, is that one's gender is not the most essential aspect of one's self and that each person must take charge of their own life and not let society dictate who they should be.

This theme of the importance of individuals is present throughout the film, displayed in the thinking of heroes and villains alike. It is the defiant bravery of one Chinese soldier that allows him to light a beacon on the Great Wall and alert the rest of his people. The Emperor mentions that one soldier may be all that separates victory and defeat for China. In one of the darkest scenes in the film, Shan Yu orders one of the two Chinese scouts captured by his horde to be killed, mentioning that one will be sufficient to deliver his message to the Emperor. Shan Yu's invasion itself is directed against an individual. Even after the avalanche, when Shan Yu has only a handful of warriors left and he can't possibly expect to exert any kind of military authority over China, he is prepared to consider himself victorious as long as the Emperor bows to him or dies. The emphasis on individual importance is highly subversive to the society presented in the film. After all, the whole point of strict gender roles is to provide an organizing principle that allows society to function smoothly at the expense of individual liberty.

The film demonstrates the arbitrariness of these roles and their distance from real people not only through Mulan, but with the men in the film as well. None of the men present are a perfect fit for the masculine ideal expected of a Chinese soldier. The most obvious example is the frailty of Mulan's father, a frailty which his pride and dedication to his role force him to poorly conceal when conscripted into service. Then there are Mulan's companions, who in addition to their initial ineptitude in their training, each represent an aberration in the masculine ideal. Yao is ugly and short, Ling is scrawny and buffoonish, and Chien-Po is gentle and fat. Even Shang, who represents the near-perfect physical embodiment of masculinity, suffers his own inadequacies when compared to the model of masculine attitudes. He is decisive enough in dire situations, but he initially struggles with his authority as captain. Not only that, but on two separate occasions he needs to be rescued by Mulan. Really, Shang serves the narrative purpose usually assigned to women in action films, that of a source of support and a reward for the hero. The film doesn't especially emphasize these traits in its male characters, but they provide further evidence as to the folly of gender stereotypes, and the cross-dressing plan that the soldiers favor over the brute strength involved with battering down the door to the palace demonstrates that they have come to understand this message to a degree.

Even though the film showcases the restrictive nature of traditional gender roles for both men and women, it is not so out of touch as to fail to acknowledge that under this system men do have greater status, or at least the opportunity for it. One of the most achingly beautiful scenes in the film takes place at the remains of a village destroyed by the Huns. The soldiers find no survivors, either among the civilians or among the army led by Shang's father. To honor his father's sacrifice and courage, Shang takes his sword, plants it in the snow, and places his father's helmet to rest upon it. As the troops move out to catch up with the Huns before they reach the Emperor, Mulan turns around and places a little girl's doll beneath the sword. She found the doll in the wreckage of the village, overlooked by the rest of the soldiers. Neither she nor the audience know who the girl was. All that is known is that she was a human. She had a family, a life, and a home. All of that has been wiped away into absolute anonymity. General Li's obligation to give all he is to feed the great machine of death is a true tragedy, but at least he is honored for it. This whole incident takes place without any speech, any dialogue at all, and there is no easy answer.

Here we see something very rare in children's entertainment. This is not the kind of education that teaches children a catch phrase like "be yourself." This is the kind of education that art is best at, the kind that expresses a complex perspective on the world. Such perspectives as these would sound oddly forced if put into simple words; they demand the creation of entire worlds to make their meaning manifest. The best films are the ones that can connect these perspectives with the hearts and minds of the audience and give them a truly enriching experience.

The word "deconstruction" is often used colloquially to refer to any subversion of a narrative convention. In truth, it means something much more nuanced. To deconstruct a convention is to break down the implicit assumption behind the convention, and thereby demonstrate its arbitrariness. To deconstruct is to take a common story, pick it apart, rearrange it and bring it together with artfulness and subtlety. All this is done not in the name of pandering or smugness, but in the name of showing that there is no one way that a story must be. *Mulan*'s rejection of societally imposed gender binaries makes it a truly deconstructive work, and the farthest cry from Disney's heteronormative reputation. Despite this, Mulan is just as homogenized and plasticized as any other Disney Princess in the studio's marketing. The *Mulan* merchandise plays right into the very feminine stereotypes that the whole film is dedicated to overcoming.

It is frankly an insult to this film and the incredibly thoughtful and skilled people who worked on it to see Mulan embossed on a pink t-shirt, or swooning on Shang's shoulder on the cover of a glittered diary. Mulan is an obvious example, but many Disney Princesses have had everything positive about them smeared by their brand. The bookish and humble Belle of *Beauty and the Beast* has been replaced in the minds of many by the highly beautified Belle of the Disney Princess line, the one whose default dress is not a practical frock but a stunning gown. The next chapter will examine the first Princess created since the inception of the Disney Princess franchise, and how her basic appeal is undermined by blind adherence to the Disney romance formula.

The Princess and the Frog

The Princess and the Frog marks Disney's return to the Princess film after a hiatus of eleven years and twelve films, although the form that the film returns to was absent even longer than that. *Mulan* and *Pocahontas* are canonized as Disney Princess films, but they were only labeled as such retroactively. When viewed independent of the franchise, they don't seem to have much in common with films like *Beauty and the Beast* or *Aladdin*. In its absence from the traditional fairy tale, Disney covered a lot of new territory in its animated films. In *The Lion King*, it brought the animal-based film to new epic heights. It moved away from fantasy and into the realm of sci-fi adventure with *Atlantis: The Lost Empire* and *Treasure Planet*. Given the popularity of the Disney Princess franchise, it was only a matter of time before Disney created another Princess film.

A fine team was assembled to work on *The Princess and the Frog*. The film has the same directors as *Aladdin*, and the style of the animation shows a great deal of influence from that film. All in all, the film is a triumphant revival of the Disney Renaissance. It has quality animation and music, and a great deal of creativity in its setting and its interpretation of a fairly bare-bones story. The film's greatest failing, however, is that since its primary purpose is to bolster the lineup of Disney Princesses it is very much adherent to the assumptions and tropes which go along with that brand. Many of the elements expected of a Disney Princess movie don't mesh well with the basic story of the film and end up appearing awkward and highly contrived.

The film is set in New Orleans and features a young woman named Tiana as the protagonist. Tiana is a talented chef whose greatest aspiration is to open a restaurant, a dream she shared with her late father who (judging by the design of his uniform) was apparently killed in World War I. As a child, Tiana was told by her father that hard work is essential to achieve one's dream and that wishing for something doesn't make it so. Taking that advice to heart, Tiana works multiple jobs as a waitress and often forgoes sleep and social diversion in order to save money for her restaurant. Despite the time she devotes to work, she does manage to maintain a circle of friends, the best of whom is Lottie La Bouff, the daughter of Big Daddy, the richest man in town. The two of them have been friends ever since her mother worked as a seamstress for a young Lottie. One day, in anticipation of the arrival of Prince Naveen of Maldonia, Lottie pays Tiana a sizable amount of money so that she will cater a masquerade ball Big Daddy is holding in the Prince's honor. Thrilled to have made enough to cover the down payment on the property she wants for her restaurant, Tiana makes arrangements to have the paperwork signed that night at the ball. Tiana and her mother meet at the building, and discuss Tiana's dream. Her mother expresses pride in Tiana's accomplishments but reminds her of the importance of love and family, reassuring her that her father's life with them made him happy even though he never got the restaurant he wanted.

Meanwhile, Prince Naveen and his beleaguered servant Lawrence have arrived in New Orleans and drawn the attention of

Doctor Facilier, a Voodoo practitioner better known to the locals as The Shadow Man. Knowing of the lazy Prince's intention to marry a wealthy woman in order to regain the lavish lifestyle denied him since his parents cut him off, Facilier concocts a scheme to transform him into a frog and have Lawrence, magically disguised as Naveen, marry Lottie in his place. In return, Lawrence will give Facilier a share of Lottie's fortune. After drawing the two into his place of business with promises to read their futures, Facilier transforms them and sets his plan in motion.

At the ball, Lottie is distraught at Naveen's lateness, and wishes upon a bright star for him to arrive. Just then, a disguised Lawrence makes his appearance. While he dances with Lottie, Tiana has a conversation with the realtors she wants to buy her future restaurant from. They tell her that another buyer has promised to pay the entire cost of the building up front, and that she only has a few days to match the offer. As the realtors leave, Tiana tries to restrain them. In the resulting tussle, Tiana falls into her dessert table and becomes covered in jelly and powdered sugar. Lottie, who is thrilled at the imminent fulfillment of her childhood dream of becoming a princess, takes Tiana inside to get her into a new dress.

As Lottie returns to the ball oblivious to her friend's distress, Tiana wishes desperately upon the same bright star as Lottie for a solution to her predicament. At this time, she meets Naveen, who has escaped from the jar Lawrence was keeping him in. Frightened immensely by the talking frog, Tiana's first reaction is to try to squash him. By coincidence, she uses a book that her mother used to read to her and Lottie when they were little girls, *The*

Frog Prince. Mistaking Tiana for a princess because of her dress, Naveen reasons that if she kisses him the spell might be broken. In return, he promises to use his wealth to grant Tiana a favor. Reluctantly, Tiana kisses Naveen only to turn into a frog herself. The two are discovered and chased away from the ball, escaping on some balloons.

Landing in the nearby swamp, Tiana and Naveen take shelter from the local predators and take stock of their situation. They agree that they'll work together until they are able to reverse the transformation, at which point Naveen will marry Lottie and use her money to finance Tiana's restaurant. The next morning, the two befriend a jazz-playing alligator named Louis, who tells them about the swamp's resident Voodoo Queen, Mama Odie. Tempted by the notion of being human himself so he can fulfill his dream of being a renowned musician, Louis agrees to escort the frogs to her home. Along the way, the group meets up with a Cajun firefly named Ray, who is in love with the star that Tiana wished on. He believes it to be a firefly named Evangeline. Unbeknownst to them, Lawrence has successfully proposed marriage to Lottie, but his disguise has ceased to function because Naveen's blood has drained from the talisman which sustains it. Needing to acquire more of Naveen's blood if his plan is to succeed, Facilier enlists the help of otherworldly spirits to go into the swamp and capture Naveen. In exchange, he promises them the souls of everyone in New Orleans once his plan is successful and Big Daddy is dead.

The group in the swamp settles down for the night after some supper and an encounter with some swamp-dwelling frog hunters. Tiana and Naveen have begun to make friends after some initial dislike based on Naveen's lazy and entitled attitude and his impression of Tiana as a joyless stick-in-the-mud. As the two begin to bond, Naveen is almost taken by the spirits sent by Facilier, but is saved by Mama Odie. The old woman tries to indicate to Tiana and Naveen that they might be better off as frogs and prioritizing love over work and wealth, but when they insist upon becoming human she explains that only Naveen kissing a princess will break the spell. She also reveals that Lottie counts as a princess, since Big Daddy has been elected King of the Mardi Gras parade. However, Lottie will only count as a princess until Mardi Gras ends at midnight.

The group sneaks aboard a steamboat heading for New Orleans, and Naveen comes to understand that he is in love with Tiana. He shares his feelings with Ray, and resolves to get a job to help Tiana pay for her restaurant. As Naveen prepares to propose, he finds out that Tiana needs a lot of money the next day if she's going to get her restaurant. Thus, he decides to go through with his original plan, but is captured by Facilier's spirits as soon as he is out of Tiana's sight. Lawrence's disguise is restored, and he prepares to marry Lottie. Ray tells Tiana about Naveen's plan to marry her, and she is thrilled. She hops through the parade, and finds Lawrence and Lottie on a nuptial parade float. Mistaking him for Naveen, Tiana despairs. Ray, not believing that the situation is as it seems since if the spell was broken Tiana shouldn't still be a frog, resolves to find the truth of the situation. He discovers Naveen trapped in a wooden box, frees him, and gets the necklace away from Lawrence before the wedding can conclude. He gets the talisman to Tiana and uses his light to hold off the spirits while Tiana gets away, but he is crushed by Facilier. Facilier tries to tempt Tiana by offering to use his magic to make her dream of a restaurant come true. Remembering the words of her father and Mama Odie, Tiana refuses his offer and smashes the talisman. No longer able to complete his plan, Facilier has his soul taken by the very spirits whose help he enlisted.

Tiana and Naveen explain the situation to Lottie, who agrees to kiss Naveen and not marry him. She's too late however, and the couple remain frogs. After holding a funeral for Ray, the two have a wedding hosted by Mama Odie and attended by the swampland creatures. When Tiana marries Naveen, and thereby becomes a princess, the kiss that the two share transforms them back to humans. The two then have a second wedding for the benefit of all their human friends and relations. Naveen's parents welcome him back into the family fortune, Tiana opens her restaurant, and the film ends with the main characters having achieved their dreams and found love.

Before a discussion of *The Princess and the Frog* as it relates to gender issues and the Princess genre can begin, it is necessary to address the elephant in the room and broach the delicate issue of race. It's fairly clear that a major impetus for this film was the creation of an African-American Princess. The use of the term "African-American" is not to avoid describing Tiana as "black," but for a precise denotation of the cultural designation to which Disney hoped to expand its market. Such a goal lends itself well to the film's historical setting. If Disney were only concerned about creating a Princess who appeared to have the desired ethnicity, it would have been easy enough to set the film in some sort of medieval African civilization, perhaps reminiscent of the Mali Empire. If Disney had done that, however, it would have made the film seem detached from the cultural experience of its target audience. Disney's efforts toward authenticity are commendable, but at the same time they carry the potential for great controversy. As is largely true to the film's time period, and truer to the present than many would care to admit, wealth and poverty in New Orleans are largely split along ethnic lines. To do otherwise would have been to gloss over the ugly truth of race relations in American history, and yet the film is still guilty of sanitizing the past to a degree. There doesn't seem to be any issue in this version of New Orleans with black and white people dining in the same establishments, and the realtors that Tiana deals with are the only characters even implied to harbor any kind of racial prejudice.

In painting such a rose-tinted picture of history, and given the relative ease in which the black characters can function within the social system, there is a danger that the film could normalize the structures of institutional racism that exist within society today. On the other hand, it hardly seems fair to insist that every film to feature African-Americans serve as a commentary on issues of social justice. It's a hard balance to strike, and there is no easy answer to how successful the filmmakers are in that regard. It is sad that this issue must even be a special consideration, but it would not do to ignore the significance and controversies surrounding an African-American Disney Princess.

It's easy to argue that Tiana is one of the best role models among the Disney Princesses, or at least that she begins the film as such. Like all Disney Princesses, she has a dream, but hers is easily the most specific. Not only is she pursuing a definite goal, she even has a plan for achieving it, and the plan is actually working. Tiana has the work ethic and business sense necessary to follow through with her aspirations. When comparing Tiana to other Disney Princesses as pertaining to her relationship with her community, Belle is the counterpart that comes most readily to mind. Like Belle, Tiana is something of an outsider whose aspirations are the subject of light mockery. Like Belle, Tiana pays her nay-sayers no mind. She believes in her dream and in her values, and she is determined to make them a reality. In some ways, Tiana could even be considered more successful than Belle. Even though she has little time to socialize, she manages to maintain a group of friends and a friendly enough relationship with her employer. She's even charismatic enough to schmooze effectively with the richest in society.

Tiana is one of Disney's most well rounded characters, and also a bold statement on the part of a studio which markets itself as a dream factory. An explicit statement that wishes upon stars aren't enough to make dreams come true is a refreshing change of pace from Disney, but at the same time it doesn't feel like pandering to Disney's critics because of the film's relatively realistic setting. Of course, the even more radical statement on the film's part is that it is possible to live a happy life without achieving one's dreams. Unfortunately, the mechanism by which the film elects to convey this message is an ill-conceived romance which implicitly endorses all the worst aspects of Disney films.

Tiana's character begins to go downhill as soon as she begins to fall in love with Naveen. The romance between the two is presented as the two of them ironing out their own flaws through the companionship of the other. On paper that's a good setup for a romance. Their initial personality conflict keeps them apart, but they find each other in the end because they have something to offer each other. The problem is that Tiana has no earthly reason to be in love with Naveen. The film's contrived reason for her attraction to him is that he teaches her how to have fun and not be so serious all the time, but this reasoning falls flat under scrutiny. For one thing, Naveen admits just one scene after his accusations of her humorlessness that he was wrong about her. For another thing, Tiana might be overworked, but there is never any indication that her lifestyle makes her unhappy. In fact, she seems overjoyed with her imminent acquisition of the restaurant. She is so close to achieving what she's wanted for years, but by the end of the film she's prepared to give up all her dreams to be with someone who has nothing to offer her and whom she didn't even like mere days ago.

Still, this relationship is framed as something positive because of the influence that Tiana has on Naveen. On the surface, Naveen seems to be a character similar to the Beast. He has an entitled sensibility because of the wealth and leisure he was born into, but he's also likable because one gets the sense that he simply doesn't know any better. What's more, he's narcissistic and thoughtless like the Beast initially is, but he doesn't have any of the anger that the Beast exhibits. He sees women as little more than a diversion or a means to an end, but he isn't interested in controlling them the same way Gaston is. Through his adventures with Tiana, Naveen learns to do things for himself and to be more considerate of those around them. This influence is certainly positive, but is problematic because of the double standard it embodies. Tiana is under pressure from her mother, and even from Mama Odie, to put her pursuit of romance before her personal aspirations. When Tiana's main contribution to her relationship is to teach Naveen how to cook and to chastise him for his philandering ways, it comes off as the film saying that a woman's primary role in life is to rein in a man's baser nature.

The message of not letting a drive for success distance one from the people one loves is a good one, but it could work just as well if the focus was shifted onto a more developed or believable relationship. Perhaps if the film had shown Tiana's relationship with her mother to be strained, her feelings for Naveen could have served as an example of a broader perspective that caused Tiana to reexamine her priorities in life. In fairness, that appears to be what the film is going for, but this idea is undermined by Tiana's choice to remain a frog, essentially giving up all of the positive human relationships she has in order to stay with Naveen. Tiana attaches the most undue importance to this relationship. She gives up on ever achieving happiness when she believes Naveen is about to marry Lottie, even though that was the plan from the beginning and she only has Ray's word to indicate that the situation has changed. She also tells Naveen that she already considers a life with him absolutely essential to her happiness, despite the short time she's known him.

It may be acceptable in a fairy tale for someone to make such a monumental life choice after an acquaintance of a few days, but this film is pointedly not a fairy tale. *The Frog Prince*, and the tropes of fairy tales in general, are well known to the characters in this world. A character in a fairy tale wouldn't have the kind of dreams that Tiana has. She wouldn't need to give anything up to be with the Prince at the end. Ruling a kingdom with a prince in tow is what she was born and raised to do. This film takes a real, full life and says that it just doesn't matter as much as finding romance. The film tries to get around this problem (and the merchandising problems that would come from the Princess not being a human at the end of the movie) by rendering her decision to remain a frog moot. Once she marries Naveen, her humanity is restored and she gets her restaurant anyway. Still, her eventually getting her dream doesn't negate the fact that she was willing to give it up in such a foolish way. Bafflingly, it also removes all consequences from her decision. The film tries to create tension by having Lottie agree to kiss Naveen without marrying him but having her be too late. If Lottie had kissed Naveen right then, nothing would be different except that the main characters would stop being frogs about a minute sooner.

The Princess and the Frog is by no means a bad film. It has good atmosphere, and a very intricate and well-plotted story. The animation quality is truly stunning, and Facilier is one of Disney's most fascinating villains. Unfortunately, the film's romantic aspect seems almost shoehorned in. Disney is trying to present a progressive and independent Disney Princess and at the same time have her adhere more closely than any Princess since Ariel to the traditional gender roles of Disney films. This sends the signal that either they don't care that her progressive character be consistent, or the character that they've worked hard to develop is subject to change depending on what is most marketable. From *Beauty and the Beast* and *Aladdin* to *The Princess and the Frog* is a huge step backward for Disney romance, and as the most recent Disney film not to mock fairytale conventions it sadly has a great deal of power to corrupt Disney's reputation. This film's utterly careless portrayal of romance and gender roles, particularly in a film that's trying to be more realistically grounded, gives credence to the notion that Disney is an insincere corporation that supports a destructive status quo in which women must base their desires and life choices around men. It may be largely because of the impact of this film that Disney is currently afraid to take its product seriously. The next chapter will analyze the film *Tangled*, which marks the beginning of Disney's parodic phase.

Tangled

Tangled is the first Disney Princess film to make use of 3D animation. In theory, the medium of animation employed has no direct bearing on the themes or attitude of the film. However, it seems clear based on the combination of 3D animation and fast-paced physical comedy set against a fairytale backdrop that Disney is trying to recreate the monumental success of DreamWorks' *Shrek* franchise. Still, it would be inaccurate to call *Tangled* a knockoff of *Shrek*. Except for the comedic elements that flavor the film, it remains a fairly straightforward fairytale experience. It features a coming of age story centered on a princess and her dream, and a common Disney conflict between love and deception.

The film's story begins with a witch named Gothel who uses a magical flower grown from a drop of sunlight to give her eternal youth. The flower also has the power to heal wounds or illnesses. One day, a queen (ruling over an area simply known as "The Kingdom") becomes frightfully ill. Her husband, hearing of the magical flower, organizes a search for it. The flower is found and its petals are fed to the Queen, healing her. Eventually, the Queen gives birth to a baby girl with bright blonde hair. One night, Gothel sneaks into the castle and deduces that the healing power of the flower lives on in the girl's hair. She tries to steal the hair, but finds that when cut it loses its power. Thus, she steals the baby to raise as her own, giving her the name Rapunzel. Wanting to keep Rapunzel hidden, Gothel puts her in a high tower and tells her frightening stories about the outside world. Rapunzel remains in the tower out of fear, and out of obedience to her adopted mother, but is fascinated by a group of floating lights that appear in the sky every year on her birthday. Unbeknownst to her, the floating lights are lanterns that are cast into the sky in hopes that she will someday see them and return.

Things continue in this way for many years, until the day before Rapunzel's 18th birthday. She has become quite bored with her life in the tower, and resolves to ask Gothel to take her to see the floating lights. When she does, she is subjected to the same scary stories about the outside world as well as a string of insults badly disguised as friendly humor. Gothel frames the discussion in terms of her convincing Rapunzel not to leave, but makes it clear by her stern demeanor that Rapunzel has no real choice in the matter. Gothel then goes off to gather ingredients for supper.

Back in the Kingdom, a thief named Flynn Rider and his two thuggish compatriots stage a heist to steal the crown meant for Rapunzel from the King and Queen's castle. Spotted by the guards, Flynn and his partners flee into the forest, and Flynn pockets a wanted poster bearing his likeness that he finds on a tree. Flynn manages to leave his partners trapped in a ravine and take the crown for himself, and to evade the soldiers that pursue him. However, he is unable to deter the pursuit of an especially tenacious palace horse named Maximus. The two end up falling off a cliff into an especially remote part of the forest. Flynn escapes through a hidden cave, which leads to the clearing that contains Rapunzel's tower. He takes refuge in the tower, but is knocked unconscious and locked in a wardrobe by Rapunzel.

Realizing that she was indeed able to handle herself against an intruder, Rapunzel decides to venture outside the tower after all. When Gothel comes back, Rapunzel requests paint made from seashells for her birthday. Gothel agrees, pleased that Rapunzel seems to have given up on going to see the lights. Rapunzel plans to use the time Gothel is away collecting seashells to go investigate the lights, using Flynn as a guide. In return, she promises to return the crown that Flynn stole, which she has hidden in the tower. The two set off for the Kingdom, but Flynn is reluctant to return there given that the authorities are searching for him. Observing Rapunzel's skittishness about the outside world, he takes her to a woodland tavern full of ruffians to scare her out of the adventure. While there, Rapunzel wins the respect of the ruffians by telling them about her dream of seeing the lights and getting them in touch with their own passions. Maximus, the guards, and Flynn's ex-partners all catch up with them at the tavern. They manage to escape, but in the process destroy a dam and become trapped in a small cave filling rapidly with water. Thinking that the two are about to drown, Flynn reveals that his real name is Eugene Fitzherbert, and Rapunzel reveals that she has magical hair. Remembering that the hair glows when its power is activated by a certain song, Rapunzel sings and the two use the light to find a way out of the cave before drowning.

Eugene and Rapunzel start to become close, but Gothel appears to Rapunzel as soon as she is alone. She had previously discovered that Rapunzel had left the tower when she encountered Maximus and feared her hiding place had been discovered. She found Rapunzel gone, and the crown hidden with Eugene's wanted poster. Rapunzel refuses to go back to the tower, revealing that she is attracted to Eugene (though she carefully avoids using the word "love"). Gothel dismisses Rapunzel's infatuation as naïve and challenges her to give the crown back to Eugene if she is confident that the bond between the two of them is genuine. The next morning, Rapunzel and Eugene are discovered by Maximus, who agrees not to arrest Eugene for 24 hours for Rapunzel's sake.

The young couple enjoy a day together at a festival in honor of the lost Princess, and a romantic boat ride amid the floating lanterns at night. Eugene spots his old partners on the shore, and docks the boat momentarily to give them the crown. The two tie him up and send him back to the Kingdom in a boat of their own. They then return to Rapunzel's boat and suggest that Eugene has abandoned her to them in exchange for his keeping the crown. Gothel, who had told the thugs about Rapunzel's power in order to set these events in motion, incapacitates the thugs and brings Rapunzel back to the tower.

The next day, Eugene discovers what has happened and breaks out of prison with the help of Maximus and the ruffians from the tavern. He and Maximus ride to the tower to retrieve Rapunzel. Meanwhile, a depressed Rapunzel notices that patterns she subconsciously incorporated into the various paintings around the tower match the sun symbol she saw at the festival. This causes a memory of her infancy to surface, and she deduces that she is the lost Princess and that Gothel kidnapped her as a child. As Gothel restrains Rapunzel and prepares to take her to a more secure location, Eugene arrives at the tower and is stabbed by Gothel. However, he manages to cut Rapunzel's hair before he succumbs to his wound. The loss of the hair's magic causes Gothel to age hundreds of years and instantly turn to dust. With Rapunzel's healing magic gone, she and Eugene confess their feelings for one another (though again they are careful to avoid the word "love"). However, Rapunzel's tears also possess the healing magic, and Eugene's wounds are healed when she cries over him. Rapunzel and Eugene return to the Kingdom and live happily ever after. Narration reveals that they marry years later.

The first thing that stands out about *Tangled* is Rapunzel's essential difference from other Disney Princesses, which is that she actually acts like a teenager. Of course, *The Little Mermaid* does a fine job of using Ariel to represent the rebelliousness and immaturity of teenagers, but *Tangled* chooses a much more respectful approach. Rapunzel is struggling not with a teenager's immaturity, but rather with a teenager's budding maturity. She's emerging into a much larger world than the one she was raised in and is dealing with very deep questions. What does she want out of life? Does she want to return home? Ariel knows what she wants and pursues her dream to the exclusion of all else. Rapunzel, on the other hand, has a dream which is comparatively easy to fulfill. For this reason, she is able to question by the end of the film what comes after her dream. This is a situation that many young people can relate to. They have some idea of things they want to do now that they have a chance to live in the adult world, but they don't really have a comprehensive idea of where their life is going.

Rapunzel's overall capability is also cleverly representative of the insecurities that come with young adulthood. Between her combat ability with a frying pan, the acrobatics that her hair allows for, and her natural cunning, she's really quite capable of handling herself in the wider world. At the same time, the film is not afraid to let its heroine experience vulnerability. Rapunzel is visibly unsure of herself when she interrogates Eugene after capturing him, and she is clearly afraid of mysterious rustlings in the forest that turn out to be just a rabbit. Rapunzel's strength as a character is best described in the truism that bravery is not a lack of fear but the ability to accomplish a task in spite of one's fear. None of Rapunzel's uncertainty or vulnerability compromises her image as a role model. In fact, it could be argued that it makes her a better role model because she's more relatable. The message that children can take away from her is that it's okay to not have all the answers and to be afraid sometimes, and that their insecurities shouldn't keep them from experiencing what life has to offer. To follow Tiana, an industrious Princess who has her dream all figured out and pursues it passionately, with Rapunzel, a Princess who is still trying to determine her role in life but whose heart is open to the wonders of a larger world, shows that Disney Princesses are not limited to being one kind of role model. They have diverse personalities and a range of strengths to admire and learn from.

It's worth noting that while Eugene appears older than Rapunzel and is definitely savvier and more experienced, the relationship between the two isn't patronizing to Rapunzel in the slightest. Eugene doesn't take Rapunzel under his wing as some sort of faithful guide and protector. In fact, early in their partnership he works against her by trying to scare her out of her journey, and the one attempt he makes to rescue her from a perilous situation ends with him getting stabbed. This instance is a perfect microcosm of Rapunzel and Eugene's relationship. Once they agree to work together, they become true partners who help each other through tough situations. Eugene holds off Maximus in a duel while Rapunzel prepares her hair for an escape. Rapunzel's hair provides light while Eugene's practiced eye searches for a way out of the flooding cave. Eugene helps Rapunzel discover how good it feels to independently pursue one's dreams, and Rapunzel helps Eugene understand the value of strong personal bonds over shallow materialism.

On that note, it could be argued that Rapunzel is playing into feminine stereotypes by convincing Eugene to give up his life of crime, and thus becoming responsible for his domestication. It's important to understand, however, that except for her ironic discovery that frying pans are actually the most effective weapon ever designed Rapunzel is hardly a symbol of domesticity herself. She's adventurous and zany, not fussy or fastidious. Not to mention, she doesn't seem to take any issue with Eugene's larcenous profession. She gives him the crown just as she promised, and doesn't ask him to return it or even ask if he plans to continue thieving.

Tangled handles the balance between the need to make the main character well-rounded and the need to have a love interest in the film much better than the one in *The Princess and the Frog*. A big part of this is that Eugene and Rapunzel have better chemistry than Naveen and Tiana, which is to say they actually get along. They might not always work well together at first, but they don't bicker and they seem to basically like each other right from the start. They have disagreements, but they talk though them without resorting to insults. So right off the bat the romance is more believable, and their prospects are helped by the fact that exploring a relationship with Eugene doesn't carry any risk on Rapunzel's part. Whereas Tiana has to give up her dream and her fulfilling life as a human (as far as she knows) to marry Naveen, Rapunzel only has to give up a life of imprisonment and abuse. Thus, the audience is able to root for Rapunzel's romance and her dream at the same time, which is not true of Tiana.

Tangled is also able to blend its comedy elements into the story fairly seamlessly, though sometimes the humor is a little clunky. One outstanding example is the duel between Eugene and Maximus. Eugene wields Rapunzel's frying pan, with which he has just incapacitated all the soldiers accompanying the horse, and Maximus wields a sword in his mouth. A frying pan used as an effective weapon and a horse exhibiting human characteristics in defiance of its anatomy combine to create a hilariously surreal image. The moment is spoiled when Eugene comments on the bizarreness of the situation as if the audience is too stupid to understand that the situation is unusual. A lot of the worst comedy moments in the film feature Eugene trying to give the film a self-referential quality. In the beginning of the film, it is Eugene that narrates the backstory about Gothel and the flower. The narration does a fine job setting up the story, but it is interlaced with sarcastic comments like "You might want to remember her" and "I'll give you a hint, that's Rapunzel." The film does feature a lot of really clever and well-timed comedy, so focusing on the bad comedy might seem like cherry-picking. However, a close examination of the comedy reveals a larger pattern of insincerity which is the film's only true flaw.

As mentioned previously, this 3D animated film which uses the subversion of fairytale tropes as the basis for its comedy is clearly attempting to capitalize on the success of the extremely popular *Shrek* films. Not that this is necessarily to the film's detriment—many of the best jokes in *Tangled* would be right at home in *Shrek*. The villainous ruffians turning out to be sensitive hobbyists, the tenacious foil for the roguish hero being a horse instead of a man, and the wicked stepmother using anachronistic speech like "Now I'm the bad guy" all spring to mind. The common thread with all of these jokes is that they subvert the expectations surrounding fantasy tropes. They provide a fun new spin on something the audience is familiar with. The difference between these jokes and Eugene's sarcastic remarks is that those remarks are trying to be funny by mocking the predictability of fairy tales and letting the audience know that the characters are in on the joke, as if Eugene is bemused that the writers have him appearing in such a cliché story where the villain is a creepy old witch.

The problem is that a jab at the predictability of fairy tales doesn't make sense when the character making the jab is currently outlining a very creative and fleshed-out twist on a classic fairy tale. The lore of this world is new and interesting and the backstory offers new twists on the archetypes of the wicked stepmother and the Princess raised in the forest. But while the audience is marveling at the story unfolding before them Eugene is telling them that they shouldn't be taking any of it seriously. One gets the sense that the film wants to put on the airs of subversion out of fear that the adults in the audience will be bored if the story doesn't poke fun at itself, but at the same time it really just wants to tell a well-crafted early-90s Princess story.

This pandering insincerity creeps into the film's romance as well. Rapunzel and Eugene never verbalize their love for each other except with euphemisms like "You were my new dream" and "I think he likes me." Of course, very sparing use of the phrase "I love you" doesn't preclude good romance. Aladdin, Belle, and Meg avoid using it until the defining moment of their relationships, the most heartfelt romances Disney films have ever had. But there are two major issues with *Tangled*'s refusal to use the phrase in a romantic context. First of all, it strains credulity that neither party would use the phrase when Eugene is dying. Is the audience seriously meant to believe that a dying man would be pondering whether he and the woman he just sacrificed himself to save are at the right point in their relationship to use "the L word"?

The other problem is that the film has no problem with Gothel and Rapunzel using the phrase. At two points in the film, the mother and the adopted/kidnapped daughter share the following exchange. "'I love you very much.' 'I love you more.' 'I love you most.'" In screenwriting, there is a commonly used trick called the rule of three. A phrase is repeated twice during the film, and then a third time in a different context in order to give the events of the film a sense of closure. There is no way to know if this was ever intended with this film, but it's not hard to imagine a script in which a similar exchange is shared between Rapunzel and Eugene. Thematically, the new context could have represented the triumph of genuine love over a semblance of love based on lies and exploitation. Think of all the dedicated lovers who share this phrase with one another, and all the gentle parents who share it with their children. Think even of Rapunzel's own parents, who have no lines of dialogue in the film but whose grief is portrayed so poignantly through the animation alone. There is something perversely cynical about the world this film presents, in which the words "I love you" are uttered by none but abusers and the abused.

Again, the film is this way not because it reflects the character's development or to serve the needs of the story. The film is this way because too many people criticized Disney movies for the shallow nature of their romances, and Disney is desperate to distance itself from this image, created needlessly by its own careless marketing of some of the best animated films ever made. For one more damning example, compare *Tangled* to *Beauty and The Beast*. In that film, as in *Tangled*, the ritual of marriage is not essential to the relationship of the main characters. Belle and the Beast discover their love for each other, and thus the audience enjoys the payoff of the film. The details of their happily ever after, like their ages and the time they spent together, are left vague because that's not what the audience cares about and a definite answer only has the potential to hurt the integrity of their romance in the eyes of critics. Maybe they got married, or maybe they lived together in the castle for a few years first. Either way, the audience sees them together and happy.

In *Tangled*, Eugene addresses the "big question" of whether he and Rapunzel got married even though the fact of their marriage many years later isn't important to their character arcs. They only mention the marriage so that people will say Disney has learned its lesson. Note also that in the closing narration Eugene expounds upon the grace and wisdom with which Rapunzel rules the Kingdom. Of course, the virtues that she actually demonstrates in the film are more like courage and integrity, but that doesn't matter. She is said to be graceful and wise because these are the qualities farthest removed from the childish Barbie dolls that Disney reduces its other female characters to in Disney Princess marketing.

There's nothing wrong with public relations damage control, but tacking on these pre-emptive rebuttals to Disney's reputation at the end of an otherwise unrelated film seems vaguely defensive and dismissive. If Disney wishes to engage with its corporate image, a better idea would be to base a film around doing so. The next two chapters will deal with two Disney films that do exactly that, but in very different ways.

Frozen

Disney's latest Princess film, *Frozen*, focuses not on a love between two romantic partners, but rather on a love between siblings. Anna and Elsa, Princesses of Arendelle, start out as fun-loving children. The two often play together using Elsa's magic power to create ice. One night, Anna's head is injured by Elsa's magic. Anna is cured by a troll, but the incident fills Elsa and her parents with a sense of paranoia. The King and Queen resolve to close their family off from the rest of the kingdom as much as possible until Elsa can learn to control her magic. Anna, whose memory of Elsa's magic has been erased, is kept from knowing the truth. As a result, she doesn't understand why Elsa is suddenly so distant from her. Meanwhile, the best thing the King can think of to control Elsa's power is for her to bottle up all of her strong emotions. Both sisters grow up very lonely, with Elsa shutting out the people she loves for fear of hurting them and Anna living without any friends and enduring a family that keeps secrets from her.

One day, the King and Queen are killed while on an ocean voyage. Despite the tragedy, Elsa is still unable to reach out to her sister. Three years later, Elsa comes of age and prepares to become Queen. Of necessity, she allows the public to enter the castle for the first time in many years. Anna, who knows that she'll only have the chance to meet anyone new for one day, resolves to meet as many new people as possible. Her greatest hope for the occasion is to find a spouse. She meets a handsome prince named Hans. As far as Anna can tell from one evening of socializing, they seem romantically compatible. Anna accepts Hans' marriage proposal and asks Elsa to bless their union. Elsa's refusal causes Anna to confront her about her reclusive ways. Under relentless scrutiny, Elsa loses control of her power and casts a magical winter over the whole kingdom before escaping into the nearby mountains.

Leaving Hans in command of Arendelle, Anna tracks down Elsa in hopes of bringing her back and ending the supernatural winter. Along the way, she makes friends with Kristoff, a practical-minded ice harvester who berates the poor judgment she demonstrates in accepting a marriage proposal from someone she's known less than a day, and Olaf, a simple-minded magical snowman. Eventually, Anna confronts Elsa in her remote ice palace and learns that she was unaware that her powers were affecting any area beyond the mountains and that she doesn't know how to undo the winter. Frustrated and afraid, Elsa lashes out at Anna and unknowingly freezes her heart. After Elsa forcibly ejects Anna and her friends, Kristoff notices Anna's injury and takes her to see the same trolls who healed her as a child and have been raising Kristoff since his own childhood.

The trolls are unable to heal Anna this time, however. The magical injury was to her heart rather than her head, so only an act of true love can repair it. If such an act is not performed soon, Anna will literally turn to ice. Figuring a kiss from Hans is the best chance Anna has, Kristoff takes her back to her castle. At the same time they arrive, Hans has recently returned from an expedition to find the princesses. He has managed to capture Elsa, who is now in the castle dungeons. When Anna is brought to Hans, he doesn't kiss her and reveals that he never loved her. The whole relationship was an elaborate ruse to secure Arendelle's throne.

Leaving Anna for dead, he lies to the assembled nobles, telling them he was married to Anna just before her death. He resolves to kill Elsa and cement his authority, but before he can, Elsa uses her magic to escape from the castle. Olaf finds Anna, still alive but in a deep despair, and reminds her that even though she might have been wrong about Hans being her true love, she has learned much about love through her experiences with her friends. When Anna realizes that she and Kristoff love each other, she reasons that kissing him might break the spell. Before she can get to him, she finds Hans about to kill Elsa and uses the last of her strength to jump in the way of his sword. This act of sisterly love causes the spell to break, and Elsa learns that love can thaw her ice. She uses this knowledge to bring back summer, Hans is exiled, Anna and Kristoff begin a relationship, and Arendelle enters a new golden age as Queen Elsa uses her magic for the kingdom's betterment.

Frozen is among the most popular Disney films to come out in a very long time. The film's most popular song, "Let It Go," is the first Disney song to become a top ten radio hit since "Colors of the Wind" almost 20 years earlier, and the movie itself is the highest grossing animated film ever made (not adjusting for inflation). *Frozen*'s extreme popularity is hardly surprising, as the film contains a lot for audiences to connect with. The relationship between Anna and Elsa is what drives the story, which makes *Frozen* far more relatable than the usual Disney fairy tale. Many viewers have siblings with whom they share a complicated or strained relationship, but very few have had the sort of romance often described in fairy tales. Further, the film offers an insightful critique of the puritanical side of American culture. There are still regions in America where an extremely conservative attitude regarding the role of women is predominant, and young girls are often inhibited by the expectations of their elders. Elsa is a perfect metaphor for this cultural attitude and also a very effective deconstruction of Disney's evil spell-casting Queen formula.

Consider Elsa's parents, who lock her up in a castle for most of her life and tell her to simply conceal and deny who she is. Such an environment might seem like the result of bad parenting, and it is, but it's important to realize that Elsa's parents are not malicious. They're only trying to protect Elsa, and they simply don't understand that they're only making things worse. The film strikes a perfect balance with regard to the King and Queen's parenting. It doesn't deny the wrongness of the oppressive environment they raise Elsa in, but at the same time it acknowledges their good intentions and their love for their daughter. With certain outlying exceptions, parents do love their children. Parents who raise girls to bottle up their passions and thoughts in order to conform to an ideal of feminine perfection are misguided by outdated social norms, but aren't deliberately trying to stifle their daughters. Still, the psychological damage this sort of childrearing can cause is undeniable. Because Elsa is so focused on being a "good girl" she has no outlet for her innermost self, which causes a deadly psychological complex. Even three years after the King's death, Elsa's father still looms large in her mind. She ponders a portrait of him as she sings about her need to conceal her magic from her subjects. Elsa has internalized her father as a law-giving figure and as a result she continues her cycle of destructive self-repression.

Elsa's struggle with herself makes her sympathetic, and makes her rendition of "Let It Go" all the more stirring when it comes. The song's popularity is well deserved—the song itself and its presentation in the film are nothing short of brilliant. Elsa finds freedom in isolation. She uses her solitude to get a better grasp on who she is and what she wants. The whole idea of the song is that she won't let herself be defined by anyone else's expectations, and yet the song stays entirely focused on what she's gained and not on the shortcomings of those she has distanced herself from. More importantly, there's a situation and a motivation behind the song. The song isn't just a celebration of Elsa's magic, it tells a story of how she came to be able to indulge in her true vocation, yet the song is universal enough that basically anyone who can relate to feelings of relief and an exhilarating sense of endless possibilities can easily become invested in it.

The visual presentation of the song makes it even better. Throughout the whole film, Elsa's body language has been heavily restrained. She's only ever stood up perfectly straight, and her movements have always been slow and deliberate. Even when she runs away from the castle she is very methodical in the way she runs, keeping her arms close to her chest. During "Let it Go," her movements are much more flamboyant. She throws back her head and sings to the sky. She lifts her arms in triumph. She runs energetically, with her arms making right angles and pumping behind her with every step. The close up of Elsa grinding her foot into the ground to make her ice palace is such a striking image because she never would have done something so exuberant back home. Elsa also lets her hair down, tearing out the crown that holds her conservative bun in place. It falls down into a long braid. Her wardrobe even changes to reflect her new freedom. Before, she wore a very conservative dress, and one that looked very tight and constraining when contrasted with Anna's short sleeved and frillier dress. Now, Elsa wears a one piece outfit that could best be described as a cocktail dress, complete with a slit up the side that reveals one of her legs. This touch tastefully sexualizes Elsa just enough to play into the subtext of casting off puritanical notions of femininity, but is subtle enough that such a theme stays in the subtext. It might seem like a bit much for a Disney film, but remember that the last time Disney put a woman in a cocktail dress the result was Jessica Rabbit.

"Let It Go" has only one major flaw, and it has to do with the visual presentation rather than the music or lyrics. Just before the song ends, the audience sees a close up of Elsa sneering before turning and slamming a door in the audience's face. The slamming of the door works perfectly. It maintains the high energy of the song and satisfyingly releases that energy in a sudden stop. Thematically, the shot demonstrates that even though Elsa has the freedom she's been denied for so long, she hasn't been able to take the final all-important step of reaching out to others. She's still isolated and as long as she stays that way nothing will get better, even if it feels better in the short term. What doesn't make sense is the sneer. Elsa doesn't view the citizens of Arendelle with disdain. She's genuinely concerned when she finds out later that her magic is putting the kingdom in danger. Her sneer undermines the otherwise positive tone of this song. What's the point of this expression? Two possibilities present themselves.

One is that the film makers want to plant a seed of suspicion in the audience regarding Elsa. Maybe we're meant to suspect that this could be a turning point for Elsa and that she might become the sort of self-absorbed villain that magical Queens always are in Disney films. For the moment, that's a very plausible interpretation. The audience doesn't yet know that Elsa is unaware of the danger she poses to Arendelle. Maybe years of being repressed have caused her to become a genuine force of destruction. Playing with the audience's expectations is fine, and if it's done well it comes off as very clever. If the film plays with the audiences expectations in a way that wouldn't make sense if the audience wasn't watching, as with facial expressions which are inconsistent with other characterization just to serve as a red herring for the audience, it comes off as cheap and manipulative.

Sadly, the other possibility suggests even less respect for the audience. The sneer Elsa flashes bears a striking resemblance to what is known as "The DreamWorks Face"—a self-aware smirk often used in posters for 3D animated films distributed by Disney's rival animation studio, DreamWorks. This face suggests to any adults who might be looking at the poster that even though this is a movie for children, they'll sneak in some jokes or situations that adults will be able to relate to and thus not be bored by watching a cartoon. Elsa makes a similar face in a lot of marketing material for *Frozen*, though in the actual film she mostly expresses sincere joy or concern. Is it possible some marketing executive insisted she make a similar face at least once in the movie to match up with the marketing? Either way, the sneer is a very serious flaw in what is otherwise a fantastic song.

"Let It Go" is a great metaphor for *Frozen* as a whole. A lot of thought and effort is put into it and the presentation is very effective overall, but it has a few flaws which at first seem inconsequential next to so much quality work, but really drag the film down upon careful analysis. To better understand this, turn from Elsa to the female romantic lead and ostensible protagonist, Anna. Compared with Elsa, who has a lot of pent-up emotion and a truly intense personal struggle to go through, Anna isn't very interesting. She's likable enough to be sure, and her fun-loving gregarious attitude makes a great contrast to Elsa's extreme self-control. The bond that the sisters share feels genuine and any scenes with the two of them together are really touching, but without Elsa to bounce off of, Anna doesn't have anything to do except be lectured to or rescued by Olaf or Kristoff.

A big part of what's boring about Anna is her persona when interacting with others. She's a teenage girl who is awkward, both in her speaking patterns and her clumsy movements. Such a character isn't necessarily bad. Rapunzel is hilarious to watch and she's the same basic kind of character. However, the reason Rapunzel works is that she fits in with the world around her. *Tangled* is an effective parody of fairy tales in the same vein as *Shrek*, and all the different characters play into that idea. *Frozen*, despite some clumsy attempts at parody which will be covered in the following pages, is really a straightforward fairy tale. All the other characters, even the genre-savvy Kristoff, still act like they're in a fairy tale. In contrast, Anna feels very much out of place.

To the movie's credit, Anna is obviously supposed to be out of place in a fairy tale in an attempt to subvert certain feminine ideals. Early in the film, as a group of nobles prepare to enter the castle, they remark about the imagined beauty of the princesses inside. As they say this, the camera finishes its long establishing pan across the town square and rises up to give us a spectacular long shot of the castle. Such a shot perfectly complements the dialogue by completing the audience's vision of fairytale perfection. We then cut to a close medium shot of Anna sleeping late. Her hair is disheveled, she's snoring and drooling on her pillow, and a lock of her hair has fallen into her open mouth. This cut is a brilliant subversion of audience expectations, which is only heightened by the contrast between long shot and close medium shot, another example of this film's flair for using images to tell the story.

Subtle touches like this scene are fine for poking fun at Disney conventions, but Anna's overall personality doesn't really address the problem if a subversion of feminine ideals is what the film's going for. Anna is a pretty far cry from perfect Princesses like Snow White or Cinderella, but she's just the sort of awkward and ditzy teenage girl one would expect to see on a 21st century Disney Channel sitcom. Replacing one feminine stereotype with another is not progress, especially when Disney has produced many interesting and sophisticated female characters in response to the classic fairytale princess already.

This is indicative of a larger problem with *Frozen*. It tries very hard to offer some skewed insight into the conventions of Disney

Princess films, but it unfairly homogenizes those films in order to prove its point. Consider the scene where Kristoff lectures Anna about the stupidity of marrying someone she doesn't know. (One wonders how he came by such insight, being raised as he was by a family of trolls who attempt to marry him to Anna the moment he brings her to their home.) He puts a lot of emphasis on his incredulity over Anna marrying someone she met that same day. His comments are obviously meant to poke fun at the traditionally short duration of Disney courtships.

Even though only three Princesses have actually decided to marry someone less than 24 hours after meeting them, this remains a fair criticism of Disney films. The problem is that those same three Princesses who decided to marry a Prince they just met are also the only Princesses that developed their relationship over the course of one or two scenes of dialogue, the way Anna does in *Frozen*. Aladdin and Jasmine's relationship might have been accelerated to comply with cinematic conventions, but the connection they shared wasn't a shallow infatuation. It was based on an exploration of their shared value systems. Even Ariel, who had nothing but the worst kind of Lacanian obsession to motivate her romance, still had to interact with Eric and convince him to find something compelling about her besides her voice.

This very criticism of Disney fairy tales has been brought up before with much more believability and sincerity in *Beauty and the Beast*. Only one mention that true romantic love takes time to develop was necessary, and it added to the characters by playing into that movie's theme of entitlement. Belle's love was something the Beast had to work for, and better himself for. He wasn't just entitled to it after one dance number. If the issue here is what kind of example Disney romances are setting for children, then actually seeing a romance realistically develop over time, even if the bulk of it happens in the course of one montage song, gives children a positive example to live by. *Frozen*, on the other hand, chooses to poke holes in a formula that has not been prevalent in Disney films for more than 50 years and accounts for a sizable minority at best of all Disney films. This is especially grating when one considers that this situation is portrayed as being a result of Anna's poor judgment. The film casts the blame on Anna when Elsa was the one who neglected her sister's need to have some form of affection from another human being in her life. Anna doesn't take off with Hans until after Elsa tells her that she will not keep the gates open after the party. What choice has Elsa left her with but to pursue a romance with someone she just met that day? Is it really fair to cast aspersions upon Anna's judgment in this situation, when she's being given the choice of living the rest of her life in abject loneliness or being cast away from the only family she has left?

Frozen seems less interested in giving children a positive example than in tearing down tropes which no longer hold sway to mollify critics. Some of these critics seem to have become so accustomed to anachronistic modern social norms in fairytale situations as a result of parody films like *Shrek* and *Tangled* that they see any fairy tale which does not relentlessly mock itself as naïve and out of touch. Perhaps the postmodern obsession with irony and self-reference has obscured from today's audiences the compelling characters and breath-taking craftsmanship that Disney has offered in the past.

It's worth repeating: *Frozen* has a lot going for it. It has wonderful animation. It has endearing characters. Elsa's development arc is one of the most interesting in all of modern cinema. Perhaps the thing that stands out the most about *Frozen* is its beautiful overall theme. The moral that love between friends or family can be just as powerful and meaningful as love between romantic partners is a very important message. Sadly, Anna learns this lesson in such a way that the application of it is left out of her hands.

Nowhere is *Frozen*'s preference for clumsy self-awareness over good storytelling clearer than in the character of Hans. One would expect Anna to understand that what she has with Hans isn't true love through her adventures with her friends. After all, this is the first time in her adult life that she's had the opportunity to form an emotional connection with another person besides her parents. One would expect the broader perspective on life and interpersonal relationships that Anna gains through her journey to let her reevaluate her relationship with Hans. Anna coming to this realization would suit the idea of a coming-of-age story extremely well, and would dovetail perfectly with the climax. Besides being motivated by non-romantic love, the other outstanding thing about the act of true love that saves Anna is that it is an action she herself performs as opposed to a kiss or some other action she simply receives.

Sadly, Anna learning the value of relationships outside of romance doesn't rely on her own understanding or agency. She only learns this lesson from Hans turning out to have been evil all along. Hans' evil is by far the most egregious flaw in this film. It undermines the moral by making it less applicable to real life, and it hurts the overall story by giving it a completely unnecessary villain and woefully inconsistent characterization. Beginning with how this revelation is completely nonsensical, Hans' actions in the last act of the film contradict his prior characterization, and his stated plan for taking over Arendelle is inconsistent with his actions toward both Anna and Elsa.

Prior to Anna's return, Hans has not been shown to be selfish in the least. He readily shares the castle's resources with the people of Arendelle, even after the greedy duke of Wesselton advises him that he's giving away valuable trade commodities. When Anna's horse returns without her, he has no reason to go looking for her unless he is genuinely concerned. His stated goal is to rule Arendelle, and the nobles state outright that if Anna should die they will defer to his authority. It serves his interests to leave Anna to die in the storm.

His expedition to capture Elsa doesn't make any sense either. Hans assumes that killing Elsa will end the magical winter. This is made clear when he gloats to Anna that he will save Arendelle by killing Elsa. It is unlikely that saving Arendelle is just a pretext for Elsa's murder. Hans has shown concern for the citizens, so if he didn't think that would work he would keep Elsa alive until another way could be found. If nothing else, he surely doesn't want to rule over a desolate kingdom and have all his subjects starve from eternal winter. If he does assume killing Elsa will end the winter, and he was planning to kill her after marrying Anna anyway, why doesn't he kill her when she's unconscious on top of the mountain and surrounded by soldiers who just fought a monstrous snow creature she conjured and just saw her trying to push one of their companions off a cliff with her magic? Self-defeating evil plots aside, Hans doesn't have to be evil for the moral to work, or even for the third act to have just as much tension.

Imagine an alternative ending in which Hans is not evil. When Anna returns, he tries to save her with a true love's kiss. It doesn't work of course, because Hans and Anna simply haven't known each other long enough to have that kind of bond even if their fondness for each other is genuine. It's easy to believe that Hans could be genuinely fond of Anna, as both he and she know what it's like to be shut out by family. Frustrated by his inability to save the woman that he believes he loves, Hans reasons that the only way to break the spell must be to destroy the "evil Queen" who did this to her. Everything else in the film could be basically the same. Olaf could still give Anna the same pep talk about the nature of true love, and Hans would still be leaving Anna in a dire situation and trying to kill Elsa.

Not only would Hans' prior actions make more sense, but it would be a great lesson for kids. Life doesn't always present us with a villain. Most of the time, interpersonal problems just arise though misunderstandings and bad choices on the part of the well-meaning people around us. That's exactly what makes Elsa's story so interesting: the lack of a villain. The King does her harm, but he has the best of intentions. She needs to break out of the shadow of her father's mistakes, first by setting herself free from her cycle of self-repression and then by repairing her damaged relationship with her sister. This conflict is so engaging because it's similar to a personal journey one might take in real life.

Similarly, Anna's conflict has no need of a villain. Which one is more likely to happen to a young woman? Is she more likely to find out her boyfriend is evil, or to simply fall out of love with her boyfriend after getting a broader perspective on the situation allows her to re-evaluate her feelings for him? Of course there's nothing wrong with warning young female viewers that there are bad men out there who will hurt them if they're not careful. That's one of the things that was so effectively provocative about *Hercules* and *The Hunchback of Notre Dame*. However, if that's the metaphor the movie is going for, it doesn't excuse the inconstancies in Hans' characterization. Narrative metaphors have to make sense in their own universe. Further, having a romantic relationship organically fall apart is a much more drastic subversion of the Disney romance formula and, as the next chapter will reveal, one that was very successful in the past.

In fairness to *Frozen*, one reading of the film in which these choices make sense must be evaluated. *Frozen*'s criticism of Disney focuses mainly on tropes which pertain to a tiny minority of Disney films, but what if Disney films are not *Frozen*'s real target? Consider the lonely life Anna leads in her family's castle. In the absence of meaningful human relationships, she turns to the paintings on the castle walls for company. Later, as she sings about the possibility of meeting the love of her life at Elsa's coronation party, she poses herself in front of these same paintings. It's fairly clear that in the absence of any real world experience, Anna has based her expectations for how the world works on what she sees in these shadows of reality.

Because of the idea of a flat image displayed in a rectangular screen, it's not hard to read Anna's fascination with the paintings as an allegory for young people basing their expectations and aspirations on what they see in television shows and movies. If this is the case, then at least the film's criticism of media affecting young minds is clever, even if it is based in faulty assumptions and blithe ignorance of Disney animation's actual products. However, these paintings could be read a different way. The paintings are not animated. They don't present a narrative or really show any interaction between people. They are stationary simulacra that the viewer must project their own meaning into. In this way, they are similar to dolls of Disney Princesses, or even random objects that a stationary image of the Princesses is emblazoned on. Sadly, while most Disney films and the relationships and women in them are really very sophisticated, the image that the Disney Princess line of merchandise sells to little girls and the public isn't. This is one of the critical problems with Disney as a company, and it clearly hurts their reputation with cultural critics. Disney intentionally divorces itself from the sophistication of its own material in its marketing, and asks us to focus on the Princesses' cute dresses rather than their fascinating characters.

For people who haven't seen Disney films in a long time, this watered down saccharine image is what Disney represents. Maybe the idea behind *Frozen* is to remind audiences that Disney films are much smarter than Disney marketing. After all, it can hardly have been lost on the creators of *Frozen* that the marketing for the film hardly matches the film itself. No one in the film makes the DreamWorks face (except for maybe that one questionable sneer by Elsa.) Then again, parody does definitely seem to be the direction Disney is headed in these days, considering the popularity of *Tangled*'s satire of fairy tales and *Wreck it Ralph*'s satire of video games. Maybe 3D animated parodies are just what Disney does now, and they're trying so hard to establish this new style as the wave of Disney's future that they're willing to throw any 2D film that unironically deals with fairytale conventions under the bus to do it.

Though *Frozen* may be unfair to later Disney films, the stereotypical Disney romance remains a prominent fixture in American cinema and culture. Even if the tropes aren't as archaic as they once were, the timeless nature of Disney films means that the films which do actually follow this formula will be with us for years to come. In the next chapter, a film will be examined which serves as a mature and balanced response to these classic Disney films. It manages to parody them and put them in a proper perspective with respect to modern films and modern times, all while acknowledging their wonderful artistry and the value they hold for us today. That film, the only live action Disney film to be covered in this book, is called *Enchanted*.

Enchanted

Enchanted came out several years before *Frozen*, but is covered afterwards here because it deftly answers every flaw in the latter film's critique of Disney romance. *Enchanted* features a stereotypical Princess character (though she technically never actually becomes royalty) named Giselle as the protagonist. She starts the film living in a cottage built into a tree in an enchanted forest situated in the magical kingdom of Andalasia. She is attacked by a troll, only to be rescued by a Prince named Edward, whom she had a dream about the previous night. The two become engaged mere seconds after meeting each other, but before they can get married Edward's wicked stepmother Narissa pushes Giselle into a magic well that sends her to New York City.

At this point the film switches from hand-drawn animation to live action footage. Giselle quickly becomes lost in the chaotic bustle of the city, but eventually finds help in the form of Robert, a divorce attorney. Robert is naturally skeptical regarding her story of coming from a far-off magical kingdom, and he becomes aggravated with her when she causes a misunderstanding that makes it appear as though Robert is unfaithful to his girlfriend Nancy. Eager to be rid of the disruption that Giselle has brought into his home life, Robert takes her to his office in hopes that his secretary can help her get home. While in the office, Giselle learns about the concept of divorce and becomes very upset.

Meanwhile, Prince Edward and his traitorous manservant Nathaniel have come through the well to the real world looking for Giselle. Nathaniel receives a magical communication from Narissa telling him to kill Giselle. To accomplish this task, she gives him three poisonous apples. As Edward continues his search, Nathaniel finds Giselle and makes two failed attempts to give her the apples. While these events unfold, Giselle and Robert grow closer together. They share their different perspectives on romantic love, and Giselle helps Robert to repair Nancy's trust in him with a romantic gift and tickets to a costume ball. She also becomes good friends with Robert's daughter, Morgan.

Some tension arises between Robert and Giselle when he confronts her with his belief that, contrary to her expectations, Edward is not in fact coming to rescue her. During the resulting argument, Giselle finds that she has become angry for the first time. When Edward arrives for her in the morning, he finds to his dismay that Giselle's time in the real world has changed her. She no longer breaks out into a duet with him, and she shows reluctance to return to Andalasia and get married. She suggests that before they go home they go on a date in the real world. Edward agrees, and the two leave Robert's apartment.

Through her magical clairvoyance, Narissa becomes aware that Edward and Giselle have found each other. She decides to come to the real world and kill Giselle herself. After their date, Giselle is still reluctant to return to her own world and convinces Edward to stay long enough to go to the ball that Robert and Nancy will be attending. At the ball, Giselle admits to herself that she has fallen in love with Robert. Narissa understands this as well, and while in the guise of an old hag she tricks Giselle into eating the last poison apple by promising it will make her forget her journey to the real world and let her live happily with Edward. When Giselle falls unconscious, Narissa's plot is exposed by Nathaniel, who has come to understand that he is not valued by the Queen and has no reason to obey her.

Edward tries to save Giselle by kissing her, but it doesn't work. Robert, acknowledging that he has fallen in love with Giselle, successfully revives her with a kiss. Narissa, furious in defeat, transforms into a dragon and attempts to kill Robert. Giselle fights her, and the battle ends with Narissa falling to her death. In a closing montage, Robert and Giselle remain together and open a fantasy-themed fashion store, Nancy is so taken with Edward's princely persona that she follows him back to Andalasia to be his wife, and Nathaniel becomes the author of a popular self-help book. The film ends with the narrator saying, "and they all lived happily ever after," a popular concluding phrase for fairy tales which has never actually been spoken aloud in any Disney movie except this one.

Enchanted is a straightforward romantic comedy that is also a parody of animated Disney films, and it serves very well in both comedic and critical capacities. Every character in this film is absolutely hilarious. Particularly noteworthy are the performances of Amy Adams and James Marsden as Giselle and Edward. These actors are able to deliver the most ridiculously melodramatic dialogue with perfect sincerity, and the characters they portray feel authentic as a result. Here we see an element not found in DreamWorks-style parodies of Disney romance.

Rather than a comically warped take on a fantasy world, we see a straightforward fantasy world that is exaggerated for comic effect but still very much as we imagine fairy tales to be. The subversion comes from the real world, which again is very straightforward. This juxtaposition of the real and the imaginary is the bread and butter of fantasy parodies, but the unique set-up of this film allows for people from both sides of reality to remain perfectly in character. This isn't to say that the characters stay in their original paradigms through the whole film. Indeed, the whole point of the film is how fantasy and reality influence each other.

Giselle comes to prefer reality because it allows for people to establish meaningful connections. So what is it that makes her connection with Robert more meaningful than her connection with Edward? One possible reading of the film suggests that Giselle prefers real-world relationships because they can only come about as a result of choices people make, and this allows for Giselle to acquire an agency she has never experienced until now. When Giselle becomes angry at Robert for the first time, she is delighted that she has the ability to so violently disagree with what he says. Just before the argument begins, she's reading a book Robert gave Morgan about important women in history. Both of these events represent Giselle's growing awareness of her ability to make choices in how she responds to the world around her.

In her own world, Giselle is largely restricted to a role of passivity, becoming engaged to Edward because he's the first man to arrive at her house. Note, however, that while she has certain cultural characteristics that make her adhere to the traditional role of the helpless and lovelorn damsel in distress, she is depicted even in the opening scene as capable in her own right. She doesn't fight back against the troll like she does against the dragon later on, but she is able to effectively avoid capture by the monster. The self-imposed nature of Giselle's handicaps indicate that her newfound agency isn't the result of some supernatural influence from the real world, but the result of a broader perspective. This hypothesis is borne out by the fact that even after she has stayed in the real world long enough to prefer it to Andalasia, she retains her ability to control and coordinate wild animals as evidenced by the rats sewing dresses in the closing montage and her ability to sew a dress for the new day out of Morgan's rug even after getting angry at Robert the previous night.

This same principle works in reverse when Nancy travels to Andalasia to marry Edward. She doesn't become the stereotypical damsel just because she is now in Andalasia, but retains her real world sass and kisses her new groom in a very aggressive manner reminiscent of Meg from *Hercules*. Here we see one of the great strengths of this movie. It would have been easy enough to have the fantasy characters behave more realistically over time as a natural result of being cut off from whatever storybook magic governs Andalasia, but instead the film makes the very smart choice of having the characters explore both points of view with an open mind and select one based on their personalities. This is helped by Edward being a perfect gentleman. In *Frozen*, Anna's choice to adopt a more sensible approach to love is made for her by the revelation of Hans' betrayal. In this film, the option of retiring to a life in a fairytale kingdom with an idealized Prince is examined as a legitimate option and found lacking.

It could be argued that Giselle doesn't really change all that much, and that she actually causes a greater change in Robert. After all, she comes to the realization that she loves Robert after only a few days and he admits that the feeling is mutual. Such an admission seems like a drastic change from the five years that he and Nancy have known each other. Still, it is important to note two things about this situation. First of all, Robert and Giselle do live together but there's never any indication that the two of them actually get married. For that matter, there is no indication of how much time passes during that montage. Some length of time obviously passes, based on the facts that Giselle opens a new store and Nathaniel publishes a book. There's no reason to assume that the romantic leads didn't wait a suitable amount of time to get married, even if they did fall in love quite quickly. Here we have a situation which cleverly celebrates the inherent positivity and possibility of romantic love but doesn't have the problematic submission to social norms that comes with insisting upon the marriage of the main characters. Robert's greatest gain from his experience is not Giselle herself, but the ability to open himself to the possibility of love again.

Robert might seem like a straw man caricature of a cynic at times, flat out saying to Giselle that a happy marriage is not a realistic goal and that the best that can be hoped for is a marriage that doesn't end. Even for a divorce lawyer, such an attitude might seem unrealistic and wholly inappropriate for someone who plans on getting married. Still, at the time he expresses this point of view his relationship with Nancy appears to be in serious jeopardy. For most of the film however, Robert is portrayed believably as a very practical and damaged man. He's nervous about the possibility of starting a new relationship, or even moving forward with one he's had for five years, but he isn't cold toward the people in his life. He speaks openly and honestly with Giselle when he tells her Edward's probably not coming because of a genuine concern for her, not a desire to show her the faulty expectations implied by her perspective on romance. He does discourage the telling of fairy tales to Morgan, but only because he doesn't see the practical value of indulging in the fantastic. He doesn't want Morgan to get false expectations from fairy tales, but he doesn't go to ridiculous extremes like forbidding her to play with certain toys or scolding her when she voices her belief that Giselle is a real Princess.

Ironically, when Giselle tells Morgan a fairytale bedtime story, it is a warped version of Little Red Riding Hood wherein Riding Hood almost kills an innocent wolf with an axe during a murderous rampage. This fairy tale is easy to miss, but it serves an important purpose in the story. It establishes that this film is most certainly a parody of the Disney product identity rather than the Disney film's themselves, since the actual story is challenging and thought provoking for Morgan in a way that none of her toy dresses are. The story of Red's rampage teaches Morgan to think about how storytelling changes depending on the perspective of the storyteller. This isn't a major theme in the film itself, but it gets the point across that fairy tales often have something of much greater value to impart to the audience than the culture surrounding them would indicate.

Perhaps this is a subtle jab at people who are dismissive of Disney films because of their corporate image and thus miss out on the thing of greatest value the Disney Company has to offer the public, their films. Such a reading is substantiated by the decidedly dark nature of Giselle's Riding Hood story. Because it involves cartoon animals, and because of Giselle's upbeat delivery, the story has a decidedly pleasant tone. If one disregards the tone of the story and focuses solely on the content, it almost reads like a fairytale version of *The Shining*. One could make the argument that this is just a case of inconsistent characterization of the land of Andalasia. After all, nothing that the movie shows of this world would indicate that such scary things happen there. It could however, be another example of the Disney image overshadowing the Disney stories. Much as the audience's view of Andalasia glosses over the more horrific elements of the world implied by the Red Riding Hood story, so does Disney marketing gloss over the darker elements that have been in Disney films from the very beginning.

Speaking of Disney's beginning, *Enchanted* is a parody which benefits greatly from being highly focused in parodying only the early Disney films. None of the Disney references in this film refer to a film later than *Sleeping Beauty*. In fact, the only films referenced in *Enchanted* are the first three discussed in this book. *Enchanted* subtly makes it clear that it is parodying these films specifically by referencing them at every opportunity. The references to *Snow White and the Seven Dwarfs* and *Sleeping Beauty* are fairly obvious. Probably the most subtle are Giselle describing her future betrothed to her animal friends based on a description from a dream, and her using a well in an evil Queen's courtyard to make a wish for a happy marriage to a Prince. Since

Cinderella has less overt fantasy elements, the references to that film are more visual. Examples include the carriage, Giselle leaving her slipper at the ball, the animals helping her make her dress, and the reflection of her scrubbing a floor in some bubbles. While the focus on these three films as a subject of mockery is obvious in retrospect, it's just subtle enough not to distract from the film itself.

Enchanted can easily be mistaken for a parody of Disney in general, but that obviously isn't the case. Even setting aside all the Disney films which have strayed away from fairy tales and romance almost entirely (that is to say, the majority of Disney films not covered in this book), the last Princess film released before *Enchanted* was *Mulan*. This is exactly why *Frozen* falls flat as a parody of Disney films. It homogenizes the entire Disney catalogue as being similar to the classic Princess movies, which wasn't true even when *Sleeping Beauty* came out. Such a mistake is particularly noticeable when *Frozen* is at the same time trying to establish its own fairy tale universe. *Enchanted* is able to strike a perfect balance by making Andalasia seem generic but also specific in terms of source material. The film's approach to pop culture references is unlike any other Disney or DreamWorks film in the last 20 years. It doesn't use pop culture to subvert the story, but just to demonstrate awareness of the story.

The best part of the film's focus on earlier Disney entries is that it would be very easy to violently distance itself from them, but it makes the choice to honestly examine their strengths and weaknesses. *Frozen*, on the other hand, feels like an attempt to mollify Disney's critics, to make a show of self-deprecation in an insincere effort to apologize for inflicting less than ideal role models upon an audience. *Enchanted* feels more like Disney owning up to their product and acknowledging that the situations in those films and the attitudes of the characters don't translate well to real life, but at the same time not denying an appreciation for those early films.

Giselle serves as a symbol of more than just the power of dreams and love, which from a real world perspective are debatable. She and the world she represents serve as a symbol of uncompromising joy and optimism. Giselle sees beauty in every aspect of the world around her. One notable instance is her awed reaction to the beauty of a statue in the lobby of the building which contains Robert's office. The statue is a stylized voluptuous female form reminiscent of the famous Venus of Willendorf. This example is worth emphasizing because it demonstrates that Giselle is capable of appreciating alternative notions of feminine beauty from those which are the norm in Andalasia.

While in Robert's office, Giselle also experiences a profound emotional upset when she finds out about the concept of divorce. Such a reaction might seem over the top, but it shows a great deal of empathy on her part for people who undergo such a painful experience. Common as divorce might be in the real world, there's something admirable about the fact that Giselle is not content to take it for granted. That incident sums up Giselle's character nicely. She is obviously out of her element in the real world, but she still has a valuable perspective to offer. Her ideas are those of a child, and the film is all about her growing up and learning to deal with reality, but never abandoning the optimism that she started out with.

When Giselle agrees to take the memory-erasing apple, she almost makes the fatal mistake characteristic of a person who fails to mature. She almost regresses back into fantasy because she finds reality too painful. Like many real people, she finds it difficult to break out of her fantasy life because she has allowed it to create expectations for the real world. Ultimately, however, Giselle is able to turn her childlike perspective into a positive force by using her vision to make the real world a better place.

One early example of this phenomenon is how she actually gets the divorcing couple at Robert's office back together. One could make the argument that this sends a bad message to the audience, that serious marital issues can be shrugged off by indulging in a childish fairytale view of love. It's true that there are many situations in which being married is far worse than being divorced, but the relationship of this couple doesn't appear to be truly toxic. When they fight at the beginning of the film, it's over custody of a baseball card. After talking to Giselle, the couple decide to work through their issues rather than splitting up over such petty arguments.

The couple are established early on as hopeless romantics, with Robert mentioning their getting married on a crazy whim. If anything, the couple getting divorced has a less mature view of love than Giselle herself. They expect their relationship to be fulfilling without any effort or compromise on their part, and all they need is for Giselle to remind them of how happy they used to make each other to conclude that a happy marriage is something worth working for and shouldn't be abandoned just because it's difficult.

Enchanted is not a flawless commentary on Disney romance. There are two minor holes in the case the film presents in defense of fairytale romance, if not as something to emulate then at least as something to reflect on and appreciate. First of all, the film presupposes the sympathies of the audience. Lyrics to two of the songs say something to the effect of "Everyone wants to live happily ever after." While it could hardly be argued that a fulfilling long-term romantic relationship is the ideal result of a courtship, "happily ever after" is a highly loaded phrase that some viewers might see as contrary to their value system. It suggests something like the fairytale version of the American Dream, and carries connotations of marriage and family, when of course marriage is not absolutely necessary in a relationship.

The other issue with this film is that it suggests Andalasia exists independently from the real world. To have things be otherwise probably wouldn't make narrative sense, but it shows an imbalance of influence between the two worlds. Fairy tales and Princesses are pop culture icons in this film the same way they are in reality, suggesting a certain degree of influence from Andalasia. However, in reality fairy tales are the product of human imagination and they say something about the values of the people who wrote them. To depict Andalasia as a world essential unto itself skews the actual relationship between the real and the fantastic. Neither of these severely damage the film, but they do serve as potential fodder for detractors.

Enchanted is just what audiences need to reconcile their appreciation of early Disney films with the gnawing feeling that such entertainment is too far removed from reality to be relevant or even socially responsible. It draws a clear line between fairy tales and real life and asks what the two do for each other. It is not only a parody of Disney, it is a chronicle of the studio's journey to modernity.

Conclusion

Disney films have grown from simple cartoon fairy tales to groundbreaking and powerful epics to clever and incisive parodies that still retain the charm and sincerity of America's favorite dream factory. This change was highly gradual, and never totally linear. For the three classical Princess films, we saw greater and greater refinements on the moving fairy tale. The stories became more intricate and serious, while the artistry remained just as beautiful as ever. The Princesses may not have been the best-developed of cinema characters, and they may have implicitly endorsed a troublesome status quo, but they remained largely positive.

In *The Little Mermaid*, we saw an attempt to update the Princess archetype. The results were mixed and the motives were questionable, but at the very least a proactive and relatable spin was put on the dreaming Princess archetype. *Beauty and the Beast* took the evolution of Disney romance a step further, by providing a well-rounded Princess and better realized characters in general. The film offered commentary on the values and patterns of the fairy tale not through comic subversion but through a serious exploration of its characters and the world as they saw it. *Aladdin* presented characters whose love was based on the appreciation of shared dreams and values, rather than the love itself being the dream. *Pocahontas* and *The Hunchback of Notre Dame* marked Disney's first attempts to bring its films out of fantasy and comment on issues of social justice. The former cheapened its message by relying on stereotypes and easy answers, but the latter met the confusion and horror of reality with the magical dreams of Disney and delivered the staunchest moral statement of any Disney film. The stories of our lives are not easy, nor will we always get what we want, but we must always hold love in our hearts and not falter in the face of evil.

Moving back into the realm of legend with *Hercules* and *Mulan*, Disney daringly addressed issues far more advanced than is usual in children's entertainment. The former raised issues of how cinema treats female sexuality, and the latter dealt far more subtly and comprehensively with the notion of gender roles than even its strongest supporters often give it credit for. With *The Princess and the Frog*, Disney presented very thoughtful commentary on its most cherished themes of wishes and dreams, even if that commentary was weighed down by a poorly executed odd couple romance. *Tangled* was the first Disney Princess film to offer the comic subversion that audiences have come to expect from fairytale animation, but retained to a large degree the serious and engaging stories associated with the Disney Renaissance. The film managed to do all this while offering a fresh take on the adolescent Princess, a young woman confused by her budding maturity and yet filled with hope and happiness at the possibilities life has to offer.

Look at the ground covered by these films. Look at the positive and enchanting characters, the thought-provoking themes, and the truly touching and inspiring romances that Disney has achieved since its early days. These are what *Frozen* is responding to. There's no doubt that *Frozen* possesses an awareness of gender issues and American cinema's obsession with romantic love, but the film implicitly suggests that the very presence of romantic love in fairytales is cause for concern. It presents Disney romance as a thoughtless flight of fancy which would realistically only lead to disaster. It looks only to the superficial narrative elements of Disney romance without any regard for what value these romances might hold for audiences beyond juvenile emotional satisfaction.

Enchanted, the only live action film produced by Walt Disney Animation Studios, shows actual self-awareness on the part of Disney rather than the pandering self-deprecation employed by *Frozen*. *Enchanted* acknowledges that the kind of love found in storybooks and Disney films is not healthy when applied to real life in literal terms, yet it maintains a clear focus on the problems of certain Disney films and acknowledges that they have endured for a reason. *Enchanted* is not a self-serving work of apologetics, it is Disney trying to reconnect with its audience. *Enchanted* tries to reconcile its audience's love for classic Disney films with their rightful apprehension at some of those films' more pernicious aspects. It tells us that we are not wrong to balk when Disney consigns Snow White, Cinderella, and Aurora to the roles of mother, maid, and lover. Still, as long as we remember that these dreams are merely dreams and do not seek to emulate their heroes, there is nothing wrong with appreciating the beauty of the worlds they bring before us or taking heed when they tell us of romantic love's uniting and redemptive power.

In a way, *Enchanted* and this book share the same goal. I hope that in reading it you have come to realize that there is value in Disney films, and that there need not be shame in enjoying them. I have done my best to acknowledge the concerns of those who find Disney films problematic, but I also hope that I have provided an alternative point of view. I hope that Disney will reconsider the cynical direction it has begun to travel. The love and beauty Disney weaves may be illusory, but it is not a lie, even if it appears at times to be shallow and empty. Each of us will decide for ourselves that most fundamental of all questions: whether Disney is a corporate monster that sells a harmful image to little girls, or a socially responsible movie studio which grows ever more aware of its own troubled legacy as the years roll on. Look somewhere in between, and you will find the steward of the American childhood, and perhaps you will find something rich and beautiful to the eyes and hearts of adults as well.

www.ingramcontent.com/pod-product-compliance
Lightning Source LLC
Chambersburg PA
CBHW021426170526
45164CB00001B/109